INSTRUCTOR'S RESOURCE MANUAL
to accompany

Faigley

Writing: A Guide For College and Beyond

And

Writing: A Guide for College and Beyond,
Brief Edition

Prepared by

Susan Schorn
University of Texas at Austin

New York Boston San Francisco
London Toronto Sydney Tokyo Singapore Madrid
Mexico City Munich Paris Cape Town Hong Kong Montreal

Instructor's Resource Manual to accompany Faigley, *Writing: A Guide for College and Beyond*

Copyright © 2007 Pearson Education, Inc.

ISBN: 0-205-55676-0

1 2 3 4 5 6 7 8 9 10–OPM–09 08 07 06

Contents

Preface   v
    Highlights of the Book   v
    Using *Writing: A Guide for College and Beyond* to Achieve the WPA
        Outcomes   vi
    Highlights of the Resource Manual   vii

A BRIEF GUIDE TO *MyCompLab* FOR *Writing: A Guide for College and Beyond*   xi

TEACHING WITH *WRITING: A GUIDE FOR COLLEGE AND BEYOND*   1
    Setting Expectations   3
    Choosing and Scheduling Major Assignments   7
    Using Informal Writing   11
    Working with Students' Writing   13
    Peer Review   15
    Evaluating Student Writing   21
    Technology in the Writing Classroom   29
    Sample Syllabi   30-33

PART ONE: THE WRITER AS EXPLORER   35
TEACHING RECURSIVE WRITING PRACTICES   37
Chapter 1: MAKING DISCOVERIES   39
Chapter 2: READING TO EXPLORE   43
Chapter 3: PLANNING A JOURNEY   47
Chapter 4: RETURNING AND REVISING   51

PART TWO: THE WRITER AS GUIDE   55
TEACHING THE AIMS CHAPTERS   57
Chapter 5: WRITING IN COLLEGE   59
Chapter 6: WRITING EFFECTIVELY   63
Chapter 7: REFLECTING   67
Chapter 8: OBSERVING   81
Chapter 9: INFORMING   91
Chapter 10: ANALYZING TEXTS   101
Chapter 11: ANALYZING CAUSES   113
Chapter 12: EVALUATING   125
Chapter 13: ARGUING FOR A POSITION   135
Chapter 14: ARGUING FOR CHANGE   145

PART THREE: THE WRITER AS RESEARCHER   157
TEACHING RESEARCH SKILLS   159
Chapter 15: PLANNING RESEARCH   161
Chapter 16: EXPLORING LIBRARIES   165
Chapter 17: ONLINE LIBRARIES   169
Chapter 18: EXPLORING THE WEB   171
Chapter 19: EXPLORING IN THE FIELD   173
Chapter 20: WRITING THE RESEARCH PAPER   175
Chapter 21: MLA DOCUMENTATION   179

Chapter 22: APA DOCUMENTATION   181

PART FOUR: THE WRITER AS DESIGNER   183
TEACHING DESIGN AND COLLABORATION SKILLS FOR WRITERS   185
Chapter 23: THINKING VISUALLY   187
Chapter 24: CREATING VISUALS   189
Chapter 25: DESIGNING FOR PRINT   193
Chapter 26: DESIGNING A WEB SITE   197
Chapter 27: DELIVERING PRESENTATIONS   199
Chapter 28: WORKING AS A TEAM   201

PART FIVE: THE WRITER AS EDITOR   203
TEACHING STYLE   205
Chapter 29: WRITING EFFECTIVE PARAGRAPHS   207
Chapter 30: WRITING EFFECTIVE SENTENCES   209
Chapter 31: AVOIDING ERRORS   211
Chapter 32: UNDERSTANDING PUNCTUATION AND CONVENTIONS   213
Chapter 33: WRITING IN A SECOND LANGUAGE   215

APPENDIX A: WRITING ESSAY EXAMS   217
APPENDIX B: CREATING PORTFOLIOS   219

PREFACE

Writing: A Guide for College and Beyond maps out an exciting journey for you and your students. It will cover every step of necessary ground for college writers, while simultaneously taking you places you never thought you'd venture.

HIGHLIGHTS OF THE BOOK

- A bold, aesthetically rich visual design that illustrates concepts and provides fertile ground for discussion.
- Detailed examinations of student writing processes and products in each aims chapter—10 complete student papers in all.
- A wealth of activities, set off in boxes throughout the book, to get students writing, revising, and collaborating, immediately.
- A "Staying on Track" feature in each aims chapter that gives students advance warning about common problems.
- An interdisciplinary focus throughout the book, tying writing to specific audiences and purposes.
- A research section that shows students why and how to do first-hand, primary research.
- Guides to MLA and APA documentation with unique "eyes-on" illustrations, showing where to physically find citation information in a source.

Part 1 of *Writing: A Guide for College and Beyond*, "The Writer as Explorer," shows students how to have something to write about, through observing and reading. It then demonstrates how writers plan and execute projects.

Part 2, "The Writer as Guide," addresses college writing as a new field for students to explore. After covering purpose, genre, and audience, this section presents eight distinct types of writing most common in college. Students are led on a step-by-step journey through the creation of each type. These "aims chapters" are the heart of *Writing: A Guide for College and Beyond*. No matter what kind of writing your students do in or after college, chances are this section of the text touches on it.

Part 3, "The Writer as Researcher," addresses the crucial element of research. Students receive advice on planning and carrying out research, as well as progressive snapshots of a developing student paper. Guides to MLA and APA documentation styles round out this section.

Part 4, "The Writer as Designer," formally introduces concepts that we and our students often take for granted: how do visuals interact with words? How do we design printed documents for the best effect? How can students design other forms, like Web sites and presentations, in which they are likely to present their writing?

Part 5, Note: Chapters 29-33 appear only in the full hardcover version of *Writing: A Guide for College and Beyond*. They do not appear in the paperback "Brief" version of the text. "Style," provides solid, easy-to-use information on the nuts and bolts of writing. Paragraph and sentence structure, grammatical error, punctuation, and English as a second language are all addressed in sufficient detail to help students revise their own writing.

Writing: A Guide for College and Beyond also addresses essay exams and writing portfolios in two brief appendices. This manual provides a detailed overview of each part prior to the relevant chapters.

USING *WRITING: A GUIDE FOR COLLEGE AND BEYOND* TO ACHIEVE THE WPA OUTCOMES

The material in *Writing: A Guide for College and Beyond* will help instructors and students fulfill the rigorous criteria of the Council of Writing Program Administrators' Outcomes Statement for First Year Composition. The skills in each major outcome area are taught continuously throughout the text, and modeled in each assignment and student writing sample. Part Two in particular, "The Writer as Guide," teaches *rhetorical knowledge*, showing students how to think rhetorically, focus their purpose, respond to audience needs, and employ tone, voice, and style. Moreover, *Writing: A Guide for College and Beyond* encourages students and instructors to employ these methods in many different formats and genres. Throughout the aims chapters of Part Two students see the value—and the how-to—of WPA *critical thinking, reading, and writing* outcomes like understanding a writing assignment as a series of tasks (in chart form, and modeled as a series of steps by a student writer). They see the *process* skills needed to draft, revise, and edit a paper. Part One of the text, "The Writer as Explorer," also covers *processes*, and makes visible the kind of flexibility and openness referred to as necessary when writing. Here students will see and practice generative writing strategies, re-thinking and re-organizing, and editing for style. Parts Three and Five of the text will give students the specific information to solidify their *knowledge of conventions* like citation and syntax.

The unique interdisciplinary focus of *Writing: A Guide for College and Beyond* makes it especially well-suited to teaching skills that prepare students for writing in other majors. Assignments and activities in the text ask students to investigate uses of writing and audience expectations in other fields, work in groups of peers to re-think their writing, and explore the value of writing as a critical thinking method—all critical skills highlighted in the WPA's Outcomes Statement.

Because the skills called for by the WPA are integrated throughout the text of *Writing: A Guide for College and Beyond*, there is little or no need for instructors to worry about "when" those skills will be taught. Virtually every assignment in the text calls on students to consider purpose, audience, rhetorical situation, conventions, tone, and genre—and every major type of writing is examined through these lenses. The purpose of each genre is also examined, so that the critical thinking skills it requires are self-evident. Finally, each major type of writing is demonstrated through every step of a writer's process, so that drafting, revising, and editing are seen as indivisible parts off the final product.

HIGHLIGHTS OF THIS RESOURCE MANUAL

This manual is designed to support your use of the book throughout your course. It will help you utilize *Writing: A Guide for College and Beyond* to full advantage, and provide advice about some of the challenges you are likely to face in the writing classroom. We have also filled it with tips, suggestions, exercises, and additional activities, expanding upon and adding to those in the text, so you have an even larger array to choose from. Good writing instruction often hinges on a teacher's adaptability: how do you adjust to varied skill levels in your class? What do you do when your students are not where you thought they would be developmentally? How do you challenge students who are already good writers? We hope the wealth of advice and options in *Writing: A Guide for College and Beyond* and in this resource manual will help you meet the many needs of your students.

In-class activity suggestions

These activities, which often amount to miniature lesson plans, are designed specifically so you can use them "cold," with a minimum of preparation. We hope they will be helpful for times when your class sputters a bit—perhaps a lot of students didn't finish the day's assigned reading, for example. Suggestions for in-class reading and writing walk students through portions of the text and channel discussion or activity to illustrate key chapter concepts. Of course, these activities may also be planned into your course.

Sample syllabi and grading sheets

Sample syllabi for use with the text are provided in "Teaching with *Writing: A Guide for College and Beyond*," below. Also included are grading sheets for rough drafts and final drafts of papers, which you can adapt to your own particular needs.

In-depth advice for teaching the aims chapters

In Chapters 7-14 of *Writing: A Guide for College and Beyond*, students explore eight specific aims they are likely to use in college writing: reflecting, observing, informing, analyzing texts, analyzing causes, evaluating, arguing for a position, and arguing for change. You may not teach every one of these aims, but chances are your students will encounter most of them during their college careers or afterwards. This handbook covers Chapters 7-14 in depth, with the level of detail you need for what will in all likelihood be major components of your course.

Suggestions for the book's *Working Together* and *Write Now* features

Writing: A Guide for College and Beyond is packed with students activities directly linked to the content of each chapter. Activities that foster group collaboration are found in boxes headed *Working Together*; activities in the *Write Now* boxes will get your students writing immediately, exploring ideas and reinforcing chapter content. When you notice one of these activities working especially well, you may want students to stick with it, turning it into a larger project or deeper investigation. Sometimes, too, an activity as it's described in the book isn't logistically possible for your class. We offer suggestions as to how activities can be expanded or adapted in different circumstances (in class instead of out of class, for example, or with a different focus, different organization of groups or individuals, etc.).

Suggestions for different learning styles

Whatever their preferred learning style—spatial, visual, aural, or a combination—all students can benefit from the activities in the book. In this manual, we periodically suggest ways to use the activities in the text so students can discover their own learning preferences. Encourage your students to try a range of these writing activities, and to notice how they may prefer one style of learning to another. They may also find that their preferences change depending on the content and the difficulty of the material. In fact, most people prefer to learn through at least two modes, and often three—for example, reinforcing a lecture (aural learning) with handwritten notes (visual and spatial). Changing methods is itself a good strategy when students are "stuck" in their thinking, so be on the lookout for chances to suggest such a strategy during brainstorming, when students need to re-think large organizational patterns in their writing, or at other times.

Detailed advice on teaching with *Writing: A Guide for College and Beyond*

The information on Teaching with Writing: A Guide to College and Beyond, beginning on page one of this guide offers specific advice for first-time instructors, covering these topics:

Setting expectations

- Plagiarism

- Collaboration and peer review

- Paper format

- Style guidelines and revision processes

- Writing center and other support services for students

Choosing and scheduling major assignments

Using informal writing

Working with students' writing

Peer review

Evaluating student writing

Technology in the writing classroom

Sample syllabi for use with *Writing: A Guide for College and Beyond*

Under most of these headings you'll find sample documents, timelines, and grade scales that you can adapt to your own particular situation. And after our discussion of each chapter in Part Two, you will find three complete sample assignment sheets as well.

A BRIEF GUIDE TO *MyCompLab* FOR *Writing: A Guide for College and Beyond*

Welcome, instructors, to *MyCompLab*, Longman's premier site for college writing teachers and students, providing the best multimedia resources for writing, research, and grammar in one easy-to-use site. We've developed a version of *MyCompLab* just for users of Lester Faigley's writing text, in which you'll find an E-book version of *Writing: A Guide for College and Beyond*, with links to unique, book-specific writing activities, downloadable worksheets, online readings, and more. In addition, students will find links in almost every chapter of the E-book to relevant *MyCompLab* tutorials, quizzes, and instruction.

New copies of this writing text can be packaged with an access code to *MyCompLab* that lets your students use the Web site at no additional charge. Please visit the site at www.mycomplab.com and select Lester Faigley's *Writing: A Guide for College and Beyond.*

Book-Specific Resources

In Chapters 2 and 7-14 of the E-book, the "My Book Resources" icons direct you and your students to a wealth of supplemental resources, including:

- Additional **"Analyzing and Connecting" questions** for every reading selection in the book provide a wealth of class discussion and assignment options.

- Links to **additional online readings** that you and your students can access on the Web along with "Analyzing and Connecting" questions to accompany these online readings provide a truly wide variety of reading assignment choices.

- **Downloadable worksheets** that support and extend the "How to Write" sections of Chapters 7-14 are helpful tools for students as they practice writing for different purposes.

- Additional **"Write Now," "Staying on Track," and "Working Together" activities** ensure students have varied and plentiful short writing activities.

- Additional **"Projects"** (major writing assignments) provide a rich source of additional extended writing assignments.

Writing Resources

In Chapters 1-14 and 23-28 of the E-book, various icons link to resources and tools in *MyCompLab* that provide students with opportunities for added practice and assistance with the writing process, including:

- **Writing Activities**. The Activities section provides 80 different writing exercises in which students respond to videos, images, Web sites, or textual prompts. These exercises parallel the kinds of writing and critical thinking expected in college. Students can practice academic writing skills, discover ideas for class essays, or sharpen their awareness of the world and their ability to reflect on their own experiences. (See "Activities" icons)

- **Writing Video Tutorials**. Interactive videos and animations that explore common issues in writing. (See "Video" icons)

- **Model Documents**. Get a head start on your writing by reviewing model documents that demonstrate the writing process, writing in the disciplines, and writing in both academic and professional settings. (See "Model Documents" icons)

- *Exchange* **and Peer Review Help**. A helpful guide for the peer review process. This section features real student video discussing successful review strategies and step-by-step instructions on using *Exchange* for your Peer Review assignments. (See "Exchange" icons)

- **Writing Process Exercises**. The Process section allows students to work in depth at each step of the writing process. They may choose to work on one specific step in the writing process, such as drafting, or choose to work through a series of "guided" exercises that walk them from one step of the writing process to the next, allowing them to bring a writing project to completion. (See "Process" icons)

- **Analyzing Visuals**. Students can learn the process of analyzing different kinds of visual texts, including advertisements, Web sites, photographs, fine art, cartoons, and informational graphics.

- **Student Bookshelf**. Link to additional supplements including a Guide to Visual Communication and the Literacy Library Series. (See "Student Bookshelf" icons)

In addition, in the "Writing" section of *MyCompLab*, students will find **Web Links**, an annotated list of valuable Web resources about writing will take them to outstanding writing guides, exercises, activities, model documents, and activities and more.

Research Resources

In Chapters 15-22 of the E-book, various icons link to resources and tools in *MyCompLab* that provide students with opportunities for added practice and assistance with the research process, including:

- **Citation Diagnostics and Exercises**. Offering content for both MLA and APA styles, this section features diagnostic assessments and follow-up, self-grading practice exercises that focus on citations for books, periodicals and electronic resources.

- **Research Navigator**. Students can access *The New York Times* archives, as well as online research tools and thousands of print journals. (See "Research Navigator" icons)

- **Research Video Tutorials**. Interactive videos and animations that explore common issues in research. (See "Video" icons)

- **Evaluating Sources Tutorial**. This interactive tutorial with exercises will help students master the challenging skills of using and evaluating online sources.

- **Avoiding Plagiarism Tutorial**. Explore issues of plagiarism, take self-scoring tests, and view sample papers, to learn ways of avoiding plagiarism. (See "Avoiding Plagiarism" icons)

<u>Grammar Resources</u>

In Chapters 29-33 of the E-book, various icons link to resources and tools in *MyCompLab* that provide students with opportunities for added practice and assistance with grammar, punctuation, and mechanics issues, including:

- **Grammar Video Tutorials**. Interactive videos and animations that explore common issues in grammar. (See "Video" icons)

- **Grammar Diagnostics**. Students can take one of the two comprehensive 50-question diagnostics to evaluate their current command of skills in sentence grammar, basic grammar, punctuation and mechanics, and sentence style. In addition to the comprehensive diagnostics on the site, there are individual targeted assessments for: Sentence Grammar, Basic Grammar, Usage and Style, and Punctuation and Mechanics.

- **ExerciseZone**. Students can take their diagnostic results to point to practice in particular areas or they can simply go to ExerciseZone and pick an area on their own. ExerciseZone includes thousands of practice items organized into 10-question or 20-question practice sets on over 50 topics. (See "ExerciseZone" icons)

- **ESL ExerciseZone**. For students whose first language is not English or who grew up speaking English as well as other languages, the ESL ExerciseZone section offers almost 1000 entries, organized into 10-question practice sets, targeted at areas most troublesome for speakers of multiple languages. (See "ESL ExerciseZone" icons)

In addition, in the "Grammar" section of *MyCompLab*, students will find:

- **Web Links.** This annotated list of valuable Web resources about grammar and writing will take students to outstanding writing guides, grammar resources, sites with additional quizzes and exercises, usage and style guides, lists of common errors, ESL resources, and more.

- **Online Handbook**. Includes key explanations of 50 of the most common problem areas in grammar, mechanics, and usage.

TEACHING WITH *WRITING: A GUIDE FOR COLLEGE AND BEYOND*

SETTING EXPECTATIONS

Certain policy issues need to be addressed at the very beginning of a writing class. Students need to know what you expect of them if they are to set appropriate goals for the semester. In addition to the usual information on class requirements, prerequisites, attendance policy, contact information (how should students contact you? where is your office and when are you there?), media requirements (Blackboard or online class site; email—how often should they check?), the policy statement you distribute on the first class day should give your students detailed information on the following:

PLAGIARISM

Of course, since you are teaching a writing class, you will be discussing proper citation methods with your students. Chapter 20 of *Writing: A Guide for College and Beyond* tells your students what they need to know to avoid inadvertent plagiarism. But your students also have a right to know the following: How is plagiarism defined at your institution? What are the penalties for it? What is the procedure you will follow if you suspect it? How can students avoid it? A sample plagiarism statement might look like this:

> **Scholastic Honesty:** If you submit any work for credit in this course that is not your own, or if you fail to correctly and fully identify outside sources, you have committed plagiarism. See section 4.2 of the student handbook for this institution's formal definition of plagiarism and its consequences. Plagiarism in this course will result in, at minimum, a zero for the plagiarized paper, and may result in a failing grade for the entire course. Note that claiming you do not know what plagiarism is does not constitute a defense against charges of scholastic dishonesty. If you have any questions about how or whether to cite outside sources in your work, SEE ME BEFORE TURNING IN YOUR PAPER.

EXPECTATIONS FOR COLLABORATION AND PEER REVIEW

If you are using these valuable teaching methods, spell out for your students how they will work, what students' responsibilities are, and how collaboration differs from collusion, a type of academic dishonesty closely related to plagiarism (see the sample statement on plagiarism above). Many activities in *Writing: A Guide for College and Beyond* are built on collaboration. They provide excellent opportunities for students to learn the group interaction skills they will likely need in the workplace after college. They also give you a chance to foster appropriate collaboration, so students know how it differs from collusion (usually defined as *unauthorized* collaboration on course work submitted for credit). Chapter 4 in *Writing* also explains peer review for your students. For more information on how you can implement peer review successfully in your class, see the section on Peer Review below.

PAPER FORMAT

It may seem like nitpicking, but it is a good idea to spell out for students exactly how you expect written work to be submitted. Must they print out their work, or is handwritten copy acceptable? Should it be single- or double-spaced (usually the latter, for ease of commenting)? What is the largest font size they may use, and what are the maximum margins you will allow? These seemingly irrelevant points can become critical when minimum paper lengths must be met. It's especially important to put them in writing if you plan to reduce students' grades for formatting transgressions.

STYLE GUIDELINES AND REVISION PROCESSES

One of the most important contracts instructors need to make with their students at the beginning of a course concerns the way responsibility for mechanical error will be shared between them. Your students may expect you, as the teacher, to find and mark all the errors on their rough drafts. However, this is a time-consuming process and, what is more, research has shown it has little impact in terms of teaching students to avoid making such mistakes in the first place. Instead, begin the semester by laying out for your students exactly what standards you will hold them to in their writing. Then explain how you will help them develop the skills needed to meet your standards. If you will use a minimal marking technique (see the sections on working with student writing and evaluating student writing, below), explain how it works to students. Give them a *short* list of your pet grammatical peeves and discuss it with them. If you are requiring or recommending a writing handbook, note it here. Your statement on style and mechanics might look something like this:

> College students and most professional workers are required to write in standard edited English. This means you must observe certain conventions, like avoiding the use of "their" as a singular pronoun, even though such language is considered appropriate when spoken. It also means you must work very hard to make your grammar and syntax help, and not hinder, the reader. We will work on this in class as we revise and edit our writing, but be aware that your final drafts are expected to be free of the following errors:
>
> - Run-ons, comma splices, and fragments.
> - Subject/verb agreement errors.
> - Pronoun agreement and pronoun reference errors.
> - Misused, dangling, or misplaced modifiers.
> - Spelling errors.
> - Inexact or incorrect word choice.
> - Language that would be offensive in a business setting.

WRITING CENTER AND OTHER STUDENT SUPPORT INFORMATION

As more and more institutions recognize the pedagogical value of writing centers, the chances are good, and getting better, that your students will have access to one. There they can work one-on-one, in person, or sometimes online with a trained consultant who will help them address the important issues in their writing. Far from being editors or spell-checkers, writing center tutors work with the student writer to help him or her identify the most pressing issues in a writing project. They provide expertise on writing techniques and give excellent, articulate feedback on all stages of the writing process. Encourage your students to take advantage of the writing center if one is available (though you shouldn't require them to go—students seem to benefit less when they do not have a choice about working with a consultant).

In addition to providing the location and hours of your campus writing center in your policy statement, consider taking a few minutes during the first week of class for a presentation by a writing center employee. Often they are happy to visit your classroom, explain their services, and answer questions.

If you have any projects that you specifically DON'T want students to take to the writing center a take-home essay, for example), note this in your syllabus.

In addition, your policy statement should note the location of student services such as the student disabilities office and student counseling center at your school, and any relevant dates or procedures for your school (for example, most documented disabilities must be brought to the instructor's attention the first week of class, or within a certain amount of time of diagnosis, so accommodations can be made).

CHOOSING AND SCHEDULING MAJOR ASSIGNMENTS

Your department or college may have already determined the types of papers you'll be teaching in your course. Or, you may have a choice of certain assignment types. Regardless of the types of papers they write, students learn the most about writing (and produce the best papers) when they are guided through a process of drafting, revision, and editing. *Writing: A Guide for College and Beyond* describes this process for students in Part One, and maps it in detail for each of the aims in Part Two, as well as for the research projects in Part Three. Plan your semester around these critical elements of the writing process.

For a 15-week college composition course, four major papers are usually considered a sufficient workload, including drafting and revision. Students need adequate time to research, draft, re-think, and re-write each project. By planning the writing process into your course, you give students ample opportunity to write and also to practice the vital revision skills all writers must constantly hone. Careful selection of the assignment types is also important. Students need an overview of the types of writing they are likely to use in college and beyond. You will have to consider your students' likely paths after they leave your class as you plan what to cover.

The most common aims of papers assigned in first-year composition courses are probably analysis, causation, evaluation, and proposal. These four assignments teach a range of skills useful in almost any college writing situation (especially so for pre-law majors). A sample syllabus centering on these four assignment types follows at the end of this section. Other combinations of aims also work well. Think about your particular student population: where are they coming from? Where will they be headed next?

Beginning the semester with a focus on reflection and observation may be ideal if you are teaching incoming, first-year students. They will benefit from a chance to put their own experience into perspective as they begin college. Students who are anticipating or already engaged in coursework in scientific fields might benefit most from assignments focused on observation, causation, and analysis (see the sample syllabus in the section following). If you are in doubt about the best aims for your students to explore, read the sample writings in each chapter and ask which ones most closely resemble the kind of writing your students are likely to want or need to do. If you don't know what kind of writing they'll do after you class, talk to your program director, chair, or a student advisor in your department.

All the types of writing covered in *Writing: A Guide for College and Beyond* can be supported by the research processes detailed in Part Three of the text. Your students will need research and citation skills in their other courses as well as after college, so plan to include research no matter what writing aims your course will address. You might assign a separate research project, or you might require outside sources for, say, a proposal argument. Remember that research requires time, and should be scheduled into the assignment. Also, note that any research paper will probably engage in at least one and probably more of the writing aims in Part Two—observation and analysis, for example. You could consider building a research paper from earlier assignments focused on one or two aims.

Once you have determined the types of writing you want students to master, you must consider how much time they need to complete each project satisfactorily. You must also think about how much time *you* will need to respond helpfully to each stage of their project. Allow a couple of days' turn-around time for commenting on proposals, drafts, and final papers. If you have more than 20 or 25 students, you may need even more time for this important work (see the section on evaluating student writing, below, for tips on how to avoid being overwhelmed by the response process). A typical assignment schedule for a short paper involving little or no research might look like this:

Week One

Monday	Discuss readings, distribute paper assignment, and discuss.
Wednesday	Students turn in topic proposals.
Friday	Instructor returns proposals with comments.

Week Two

Monday	Students submit rough drafts and engage in peer review.
Wednesday	Instructor returns drafts with comments and discusses common problems/successes; students exchange peer reviews and discuss.
Friday	Students work in class on revising papers, or do other projects related to the paper (reading other examples of this type of writing, for example, and analyzing them).

Week Three

| Monday | Students submit revised drafts for final grade. |

Depending on how often your class meets, the length of the paper, and the overall difficulty of the assignment, you might want to give students more than one class day in between receiving rough draft comments and submitting their final drafts (a weekend is always nice).

Another factor is the number of steps you have broken the project into (this technique is sometimes referred to as platforming). Breaking an assignment into discrete chunks helps students master one skill at a time and then combine them into a finished project. This is especially helpful for papers that teach a number of disciplinary skills and count for a substantial portion of the course grade. An assignment schedule for a longer paper with a significant research component, where groups write a paper together and then present their findings to the class, could look something like this:

Week One

| Tuesday | Distribute paper assignment, discuss, assign groups, and brainstorm research areas. |
| Thursday | Students bring preliminary research plans to class and discuss with groups. |

Week Two

Tuesday	Groups submit topic proposals and research plans.
Thursday	Instructor returns proposals and plans with comments. Students work in class discussing or investigating topics related to the project.

Week Three

Tuesday	Groups submit annotated bibliographies and presentation outlines.
Thursday	Instructor returns bibliographies and outlines with comments.

Week Four

Tuesday	Students work in class discussing or investigating topics related to the project.
Thursday	Groups submit drafts of papers.

Week Five

Tuesday	Instructor returns paper drafts with comments.
Thursday	Groups work in class on paper revisions.

Week Six

Tuesday	Groups spend some class time fine-tuning presentations.
Thursday	Final drafts due; groups present on their topics.

The proposal-draft-revision steps described here are well-tested and give good results for many kinds of projects. However, you can sequence or platform assignments in other ways, too. If you want students to analyze a short editorial, for example, you might have them begin by writing a short, impartial summary of it that they can then incorporate into their analysis. This sequence encourages them to look for all salient elements of the editorial, rather than just those they initially react to. The first time you try sequencing a particular assignment, it's a good idea to build a little flexibility into the schedule, in case some segments turn out to require more or less time than you anticipated.

An important note: don't take too long before returning graded final drafts. Even though students won't be revising them, they need timely feedback on their final effort to see what worked and what didn't. Then too, students often perceive instructors who take weeks to grade and return assignments as disrespectful—and rightly so. If you want them to take their writing seriously, your actions should demonstrate that *you* take it seriously, too.

USING INFORMAL WRITING

What will your students be doing when they aren't writing their "big" papers? *Writing: A Guide for College and Beyond* gives you many productive and fun options around which to structure your course. In and out of class, students might look for other examples of the type of writing they are studying; seeing how reflection is used, for example, in Humanities writing, popular media, and formal speeches. They might do research into writing formats in various disciplines. They may do informal writing that helps them re-think their larger writing projects. They may venture out into their campus or town to find subjects, data, or organizational possibilities for their writing. They may work with peers and in groups for many of these activities.

Mixing informal with formal writing is the best way to teach writing, critical thinking, and content. Allowing students to work with complex new ideas informally, in various modes like writing, discussion, and even doodling, produces the best results in terms of mastery and retention. You can use informal writing to begin or refocus class discussions, to explore new concepts, to help students re-think work they have already done and see it in new terms. The interweaving of both kinds of writing throughout *Writing: A Guide for College and Beyond* should help you understand the benefits of such an approach. But by all means, don't take our word for it. Try it in your class and see how your students respond. We are confident they'll see themselves making more progress, and struggling less to comprehend concepts.

Try rotating activities like these on a daily basis: working in class on portions of major assignments; discussing where students are in their work; writing informally to jump-start discussion of readings; conducting research (online in networked classrooms); working in small groups to answer questions, brainstorming lists, etc.; discussing writing as a class—for example, putting a few sentences from each student's draft on an overhead and talking about how they can be clarified or strengthened.

WORKING WITH STUDENTS' WRITING

You may initially be taken aback by the amount of work your students' papers need in the area of grammar and mechanics. Regardless of their skill level, students' mechanical skills will often regress somewhat when they encounter the new ideas, demands, and deadlines of college writing. Rest assured that they can all improve their control of style and mechanics—but that such progress cannot happen independently of their progress in organizational and critical thinking. They key to really improving students' writing is to focus your instructional energy where it will do the most good. In terms of writing skills, research has shown that the following methods are effective ways to improve student writing at all levels:

- Face-to-face conferencing over pieces of the students' own writing. This can take place in your office, in a writing center, or during times you schedule into your class.

- Addressing mechanical and grammatical errors in the context of students' own writing. You might, for example, have students bring in a troublesome passage in a draft they are working on, copy these with names removed, and distribute to the entire class for discussion.

- Prioritizing concerns from large-scale issues (content, thesis, organization, logic, evidence) to small-scale ones (stylistic choices, grammatical errors, spelling). Help students first with the global issues that impair their writing. As they begin to organize and fine-tune their ideas, they will usually develop (with your help) the syntactical tool they need to express them. But having students perfect the grammar of vapid writing does no one any good.

- Giving students direct experiences with multiple audiences. There are many ways of doing this, such as having students personally define their audience for each assignment, undertaking service learning projects, or practicing peer review (see below).

Many beginning writing instructors are surprised to learn that the following instructional techniques, while not necessarily *ineffective* (depending upon how they are employed), result in far less learning, when compared to the effort they require of the teacher. Experienced writing instructors, however, are seldom surprised. They may have spent years attempting to teach with these methods, and seen first-hand the relatively poor results:

- Completing grammar exercises from handbooks, stripped of any context or relation to the students' own work.

- Line-editing student papers, marking and correcting their errors for them. While this often results in cleaner final papers, it teaches students to rely on the instructor to find error. It also causes students to focus on small-scale issues to the extent that they never even consider making large-scale changes to the organization or content of their writing—even when such changes are sorely needed.

13

- Grading early drafts of formal writing. Though students may need some kind of credit attached to their early drafts, to convince them they are important, attaching a letter grade to this work often interferes with the revision process. Students who get very low grades on early drafts may feel helpless and give up any attempt to revise, while those who receive high or satisfactory grades may not see a need to improve the work. Instead, offer revision-oriented feedback on these drafts. See the section on Evaluating Student Writing, below, for more information on how to provide early feedback without grading.

If you focus your efforts on pedagogical methods that have been shown to improve student *learning*, you and your class will probably experience less frustration during the semester. You will also have the rewarding experience of seeing real development in their writing and thinking skills.

PEER REVIEW

In an art classroom, students work on their drawings, paintings, or sculptures in a large common studio, often taking breaks to walk around and view their peers' work. This gives them the benefit of multiple perspectives, and provokes questions very helpful to the developing artist: How did my fellow students approach this project? How did they try to solve the problems or answer the questions I am grappling with? What techniques did they use that were successful? Which were not successful? Which of their techniques might I employ or adapt in my own work?

In the writing classroom, such peer critique is just as beneficial, both for the improvement of the written product and for the development of writing skills. Student writers benefit as much or more from articulating their criticism of others' work as they do from receiving such criticism. However, writers work differently from painters and sculptors, so their peer review can't be as spontaneous. Instead, it must be arranged, planned, and practiced if you and your students are to receive its full benefit. Many, many systems for arranging peer review of student writing exist; a cursory Internet search will introduce you to them. Almost all involve students discussing each other's papers, often reading them aloud (reading one's own work helps in the identification of mechanical error especially), and then responding in writing to a series of questions or concerns. We also provide two methods for implementing peer review, including student handouts explaining each process, below. Either one might work for your class, or you might combine or adapt them. You should choose a method you think is likely to work well with your students and your schedule. Here are some important considerations when devising a method for peer review:

1) The overall maturity of your students, as students and as writers. Do they have experience giving and taking criticism constructively? Can they meet deadlines? Will they work responsibly in groups, or will they need a lot of supervision? This will affect how much time you allow for review, how large your groups are, and whether students work in class or at home (or both).

2) How varied is the level of writing skill in your class? Are some students much more advanced writers than others? This will affect how you set up groups.

3) Do you have non-native English speakers in your class? They will usually benefit greatly from peer review, but may be less confident in their ability to contribute constructive criticism of others' work. Note that native speakers often gain a much better understanding of grammar and syntax when they try to explain it to non-native speakers.

However you choose to do your peer review, it is an excellent plan to conduct a "dry run" before the first one. Distribute to students your guidelines and a sample essay that a previous student has given you permission to use (in a pinch, you can even write the essay yourself—a very good way to check the difficulty of the assignment!). Then, walk the class through the questions you want them to consider as they review their peers' drafts. This is a great way to get students talking about what a piece of writing does well or poorly. It also gives you an opportunity to coach them on how to articulate criticism respectfully as well as productively. And it may give you a better understanding of how sophisticated they really are about discussing writing.

PAIRED PEER REVIEW

The first process described in the following pages was developed for a second-year Humanities class where students did a fair amount of independent work. The paper assignment required them to describe an example of stereotyping or ethnocentrism they had experienced and analyze it according to the concepts covered in the class. They were put into pairs, with the goal being a rough match of writing ability between partners. At other times, you might want to pair advanced and poor writers, but beware of situations where the weaker writer comes to rely on the stronger one—this creates resentment among the more competent writers, who do not receive criticism that is as helpful as that which they give. Note that the criteria the instructor will use to evaluate the peer reviews are included with the instruction sheet. Attaching some kind of grade value to the process of peer review will keep it from becoming a thoughtless exercise for students.

GROUP PEER REVIEW

The second of the two peer review processes that follow involves two in-class interactions rather than the one employed for the paired peer review above. It was used in a first-year composition class where students had little prior experience working in groups. They were placed in groups of four or five and reviewed drafts consisting of two summaries of advertisements, followed by a comparative analysis. The groups were monitored in class to ensure participation. With this method, students benefit from seeing at least three other people's essays, and receiving feedback from multiple perspectives. This reduces the impact of any unhelpful reviews. Note again the inclusion of grading criteria, so students know what is expected of them in their review.

Due date for take-home portion: Tuesday, September 9

In-Class Reading and Review

You will work in pairs, which I will assign. The person who wrote the paper should begin by reading it aloud; then you will all discuss how it might be improved. The writer should also mention any particular concerns he or she has about the essay at this point.

When you are reading:

1) Take note of how your essay sounds as it is read — this is often the best way of finding mechanical problems in your writing.

2) Make notes as you go along, marking anything you wish to discuss with your partner.

When you are listening:

1) Make note of places where you are confused by what you hear. Discuss these points with the writer. How can they be made clearer?

2) Ask yourself if the writer seems to understand and correctly use the concepts from the reading and the classroom discussion.

3) Do you agree with the way the writer has interpreted the example he or she is describing? Do you think the writer could say more about the example?

Take-Home Assignment: Writing A Peer Response

After both essays have been read and discussed, swap papers so that each of you takes one home to review. You may use the rest of class time to begin drafting your response, discussing it with the writer when you have questions. You will write a two-page response (typed, double-spaced, and proofread) addressed to your peer. Put your name and the name of your peer on your response. Your comments, to be helpful to your classmate, must be specific and honest. Be polite, but remember that it is not helpful to tell your peer that everything about his or her essay is wonderful. You are not judging the essay, or speculating about what grade it deserves. You are simply engaging in a discussion with the writer about the essay. Ask yourself:

1) How interesting is the essay, overall? What was interesting about it? What would make it more interesting?

2) Were there parts where you got confused or didn't understand what your peer was trying to say? Tell him or her where those places were.

3) How well does the essay develop its topic? That is, what does it tell you about the example of stereotyping or ethnocentrism that you might not have seen yourself?

4) What are the strengths of the essay at this stage? If this was your draft, what would you change about it?

5) Point out any problems you see with grammar, spelling, or punctuation. Resist the urge to fix these for your peer. Just mark them or mention them. If there were enough problems to make the essay hard to read, say so.

6) Bring **two copies** of your report to class on **Tuesday, September 9**, give one copy to me, and give the other copy, with the draft you reviewed, back to your peer.

Grade Scale for Peer Responses (points out of 10):

These are the criteria I will use to grade your review:

9-10: Excellent response that really gives the writer a sense of the essay's strengths and weaknesses. Offers detailed, helpful advice, with specific suggestions, but does not provide "answers"; instead, the responder asks questions that help the writer see the essay from the reader's point of view.

7-8: Thorough, helpful review. Goes into some detail about the essay's strengths and weaknesses. Makes specific suggestions about possible improvements.

4-6: Response offers useful advice but may lack thoroughness or detail, or miss some important problem in the essay.

1-3: Response is of little or no practical help to the writer. Responses like "Everything looks good to me!" or "Great job!" or "I can't find any mistakes," fall into this category.

Paper # 1 Peer Evaluation
Instructor Name, Class

Due date for take-home portion: Wednesday, February 17

To do at home:

Before you leave class today, exchange papers so that you have a copy of each group member's essay, and each member has a copy of yours. Please put your name on your copy of each classmate's paper. Each person should take a turn expressing his or her concerns about the paper at this stage, and noting any particular aspects he would like reviewers to focus on.

Take all your peers' drafts home and write a 1-page review of it, using the approach we practiced in class: considerate, honest, and specific. Consider the following questions:

1. What is the writer's claim or thesis? Could it be clearer or more interesting?

2. Are the summaries clear and do they provide all the information needed, without being too long? What parts of the summaries need work?

3. Is the analysis in the paper logical? Does the writer provide evidence from the ad to back up his or her claims? What parts of the analysis need work?

4. Does the overall organization of the paper work well? How might it be improved?

5. Indicate on the paper any places you think the writer needs to give more information, like specific details, evidence, reasons, etc. Mark any areas (sentences, phrases) that are not clear to you. You can mark grammatical and spelling errors, but do not correct them.

Bring all the reviews you have written back to class on **Wednesday**, and return them, along with the draft copies, to your partners. You will receive three or four reviews of your essay at that time. Here is the process we will follow on Wednesday:

In-Class Peer Critique:

1. Discuss the papers one at a time, allowing the writer time to ask questions about the reviews he or she has received.

2. Each student in a group should comment on each paper. Everyone participates; I will come around the room to make sure this happens.

3. Do not judge or rank papers. Do not discuss grades. If you wish, you may refer to the grading criteria on the paper assignment sheet as you discuss particular elements of a paper.

4. Take home all the reviews written for you and use them, along with my comments on your draft, to revise your paper. When you hand in your final draft, you must also hand in all the reviews written for you so I can grade them and return them to their authors.

The grading criteria for the reviews are as follows (points out of 5):

5: Response offers detailed advice addressing the concepts and overall organization of the work as well as stylistic and mechanical concerns. Provides specific illustrations of what the author does well and how these strengths could be expanded throughout the paper.

4: Response is thorough and provides insightful comments on the quality of the writing, what it does well, and how it could be improved. Addresses issues like claims, evidence, and support. Gives an idea of what it was like to read the essay. Positive remarks about the work are specific (e.g., "I liked your use of visual detail on page two, to describe the scene").

3: Response offers some useful suggestions but may lack thoroughness or detail. Spends more time on small issues like grammar than on structure, organization, and ideas in the work.

2: Response offers generic advice or consists mostly of personal opinions (e.g., "I thought this was really good").

1: Response offers little or no helpful advice and does not point out anything about the essay that is not obvious. Or, the response is missing something very important about the essay, such as a failure to address the assigned topic.

EVALUATING STUDENT WRITING

The section on Working with Student Writing, above, describes some of the pitfalls to avoid when evaluating your students' work. Generally, your comments on student writing will have the biggest impact if they come at a time when students can still use them to improve their paper grade. So, when you comment on early drafts, help the student set revision goals. Prioritize the areas of the paper that need strengthening.

ROUGH DRAFTS

Commenting on drafts can become time-consuming, and it is easy to fall into the line-editing habit as you go along. Often you'll find yourself repeating a few comments over and over again on multiple papers. To streamline this task and ensure parity in the amount of time each paper receives, you can use a comment sheet in conjunction with other comments (on the draft itself, via email, or in conference). The rough draft comment sheet should be keyed to the grading criteria for the assignment (we'll discuss criteria momentarily), and, like the criteria, it should prioritize higher-order concerns. You can adjust the items on the sheet as you gain experience, to highlight the most common problems. However you set up your comment sheet, leave some blank space for individualized comments. There is a sample rough draft comment sheet at the end of this section.

FINAL DRAFTS

It's important to comment on final, graded drafts of papers too, but you should be providing a different kind of feedback at that stage. Rather than suggesting revision strategies, focus on what the student should keep in mind as he or she begins the next project.

You'll find grades much easier to assign, and much easier for students to understand, if you base them on clear criteria. Provide specific grading criteria *in writing* for each assignment—either at the beginning of the semester in a generic rubric, or on each assignment sheet (you can also combine these methods, adding to the assignment sheet just the criteria specific to that assignment). Prioritize criteria so that higher-order concerns like thesis, logic, and evidence come first on the list and, ideally, carry the most weight grade-wise. Your institution may have formal criteria for all first-year writing classes, or a description of writing competencies in the student handbook. These can either be printed out for students just as they are, or perhaps adapted for your class.

For individual assignments, make sure the criteria explain the way you want the assignment to be realized, and don't just repeat the assignment. For example, if an assignment asks students to describe as part of the writing task, the criteria might stipulate that "vivid, concrete description, using specific details and giving readers a clear picture of the object" will warrant the highest marks. Simply saying "I will grade your paper according to how good your description is" does not give students any new information.

Discuss grading criteria with your students before beginning an assignment. Use a sample essay to identify earmarks of each criterion: What does a "strong thesis" look like, as opposed to a "weak" one? What does "poor word choice" mean? Show students examples of each trait. See what they think good, mediocre, and poor responses look like. You will probably be surprised at how high their standards are.

Using and discussing grading criteria will result in fewer questions about paper grades. It will also make grading a teaching tool, not just a yardstick. Considering how much effort we put into grades, and how much emphasis students place on them, it makes sense to employ them so that they actually teach your students something.

Several samples of grading criteria and grade sheets follow at the end of this section.

PORTFOLIOS

Portfolio assessment is an especially appealing method of assessment for writing instructors. The scope of this book does not permit extensive discussion of writing portfolios, but many excellent books on the subject are available; your school may also have information on portfolio options for instructors.

Writing students benefit from portfolios because the ongoing collection of their work makes evident both the amount of work they have invested and the amount of progress they have made. Instructors benefit form portfolios for the same reason, and also because the evidence presented in a portfolio demonstrates a student's actual development as a writer—not just the skills he or she brought into the class at the beginning. This better enables you to assess the effectiveness of your teaching.

To work well, portfolios must have clear goals and procedures. *Writing: A Guide for College and Beyond* contains an appendix addressing portfolios from the students' point of view. You may find this information helpful as you research the types of portfolios you could use in your writing class.

ESSAY EXAMS

If you use in-class essays to assess your students' writing skills, you should still follow the basic advice we have given here: make your expectations clear in the assignment and provide written criteria you will use to assess the essay. It is also a good idea to give students a sense of the essay's purpose: are you assessing their comprehension of course material? Are you modeling the kind of writing they may do under pressure in the workplace some day?

Writing: A Guide for College and Beyond contains an appendix addressing essay exams from the students' point of view. You may find this information helpful as you construct essay questions for your students. Students will, of course, write many such essay exams in college; remember, however, that essay exams are better at assessing writing skills than improving them. The more time your students spend on essay exams, the less time they will have to practice the critical skills of brainstorming, research, revision, and editing.

Paper Assignment # 4: A Practical Proposal

Choose a problem that you have experience with and write a practical proposal to solve the problem. To find a topic, consider problems at this institution; your high school; your city or town; your place of work; etc. Brainstorm to find a narrow, local issue which is a problem for you. Describe in detail what the issue and what the problem is—you need to convince your audience that the problem exists and that it's worth addressing.

Describe in detail how this solution works: how much money it will cost, who will be responsible for implementing it, how easily it can be implemented, how much time it will take to set it up and make it work, what kinds of materials and labor are needed to make it work, etc. Use your own research (interviews, surveys, graphs, polls) and/or library research. Document your sources accurately, both in your text and in a Works Cited page using MLA format. You must use at least four outside sources.

Justify your solution: give reasons for enacting the proposal (other than those which relate to its being able to solve the problem—think of audience-based appeals and other appeals to pathos here) and convince your audience that the solution should be enacted and is worth enacting.

Your paper should be four to five pages long, typed, double-spaced, and carefully proofread. You must cite at least four outside sources, at least two of which must be unavailable online. You should use MLA guidelines for formatting and include a Works Cited page. Be forewarned that I will spot-check both Internet and library sources, so you may wish to photocopy any materials you will be using that are not available online.

Grading Criteria

In addition to the general grading criteria described in the course syllabus, which apply to all papers in this class, I will evaluate your essay according to three specific criteria:

1) your description of the problem, and the degree to which you make it seem truly worth addressing

2) the specificity and feasibility of your proposal

3) the quality of the evidence you marshal in support of your argument

Due dates

Friday, July 24 - topic proposal due
Friday, July 31 - first draft due with copies for peers
Monday, August 3 - peer reviews due
Wednesday, August 5 (last class day) - final draft due

Rough Draft Comment Sheet — Analysis and Refutation of a Text

Consult your draft for additional comments, and refer to the assignment sheet for more specific information about the criteria for this project. You are expected to use your grammar handbook as a tool during revision. For maximum benefit, meet with me and/or a Writing Center Consultant to discuss your draft.

Work on . . .		
your basic claim		You have not taken a position that effectively refutes your chosen essay.
		You are not addressing the same audience your opponent is addressing.
		Other:
logic and critical analysis		There are logical inconsistencies or fallacies in your argument.
		You fail to adequately address some of your opponent's most important points.
		Other:
structural development		Some sections of the essay do not directly support your thesis.
		The content of some paragraphs does not support the topic sentence.
		Other:
evidence and supporting reasons		You need to provide more specific evidence and/or reasoning to back each of your claims.
		You need to find more effective strategies for countering your opponent's evidence.
		Other:
style and mechanics		Your sentences have structural problems that hinder the reader. See example on page ____
		Vocabulary, clarity, and/or word choice need work. See example on page ____
		The essay has basic problems with spelling, punctuation, and grammar. See example on page ____
		Other:

Additional comments:

Holistic Grading Rubric Example #1

These criteria will apply to all major papers written in this class.

A "C" paper will:

- be the student's own independent work (peer review and assigned collaboration excepted).
- meet all the specific requirements of the assignment, including format, length, and due date.
- have an identifiable thesis or topic.
- provide sufficient evidence to support any claims it makes.
- correctly document, through citation, accurate quotation, or correct summary and paraphrasing, its outside sources, if any.
- have at least a basic structure that moves the central idea forward from the introduction to some kind of conclusion that does not merely repeat what has been already said.
- use transitions to appropriately link its ideas.
- demonstrate understanding of the learning goals for the unit (keys of observational writing, etc.).
- demonstrate understanding of the audience addressed, and the purpose for writing.
- actively respond to feedback from the instructor and from peers (not just fixing mistakes, but re-thinking ideas, structure, and other large-scale issues to improve the piece).
- have grammar and syntax that do not impede the reader's progress through the paper.

A "B paper will:

- do everything a "C" paper does.
- have an interesting and clear thesis or topic.
- provide a range of convincing evidence, from a variety of sources.
- quote and paraphrase so that readers can easily follow the transition from the author's thoughts to those of outside experts.
- have an organizational pattern that strongly supports a fairly complicated set of ideas, and moves readers from an interesting opening to a satisfying conclusion.
- use transitions to show subtle relationships between ideas.
- demonstrate mastery of the learning goals for the unit.
- demonstrate a through understanding of the audience addressed, and the purpose for writing, using specific tone and language to address them.
- actively respond to feedback and show initiative in finding ways to improve the writing.
- have grammar and syntax that actively help the reader through the paper.

An "A" paper will:

- do everything a "B" paper does.
- have a provocative or surprising thesis.
- provide an impressive array of evidence from a wide range of sources.
- quote and paraphrase seamlessly, giving the impression of a fluid conversation among several parties.

- have a complex but clear organizational pattern that springs from but also supports the ideas, with an opening that invites readers in and a conclusion that moves them in some way.
- use transitions to help readers confidently negotiate complex ideas.
- demonstrate mastery of the learning goals, and a willingness to go beyond the basic knowledge covered to learn more.
- demonstrate thorough understanding of audience and purpose, and an ability to appeal to a perhaps hostile or indifferent audience.
- respond to feedback by applying broad suggestions across the entire paper.
- have grammar and syntax that make the paper enjoyable to read, and make the reader feel smart.

A "D" or "F" paper will have failed to meet the minimal requirements for a "C."

Holistic Grading Rubric Example #2

These criteria will be used to grade all your papers for this class. In addition, you will find criteria specific to each assignment on the assignment sheet.

Content and Structure
- An excellent paper will provide outstanding content that interests the reader, and organize it according to an appropriate plan that helps the reader along.
- An average paper will provide good content and use a reasonable plan to organize it. It will not bore the reader, but may be a little less satisfying or a little harder to read than an excellent response.
- A below-average paper will not provide enough content and will either use a basic structure that does not really fit the content, or not have a structure at all.

Logic and Evidence
- An excellent paper will make strong logical arguments, providing a convincing array of outside evidence.
- An average paper will make reasonable arguments, but may miss some important objections. It will provide strong support from outside sources, but may not convince its readers.
- A below-average paper will make arguments that are illogical or contain fallacies. It will have insufficient supporting evidence to convince the reader.

Style and Tone
- An excellent paper will make stylistic choices that render the paper a pleasure to read. The tone will be appropriate to a specific audience.
- An average paper will be easy to read. The tone may be somewhat "toneless": not offensive to the audience, but not particularly directed at any one audience either.
- A below-average paper may lack real style. It may suffer from poor word choice or wordiness. It will either address the wrong audience or use a tone that is not likely to engage the audience.

Grammar and Mechanics
- An excellent paper will have grammar and mechanics that do all the work for the reader. No matter how complicated the ideas, the paper's mechanics will guide the reader safely through.
- An average paper will have strong grammar and mechanics that never get in the way of the reader's journey.
- A below-average paper will have grammar and mechanics that trip the reader up frequently and make it hard to understand what the author means.

Quantitative Grading Rubric

See your assignment sheet for more detailed explanations of each of the categories below.

Area:	Comments:	Points earned:
Ideas and their structure (25 points)		
Clear thesis (5)		
Logic and development of ideas (10)		
Overall structure and transitions (10)		
Supporting evidence (25 points)		
Quality/quantity of sources (10)		
Anticipation of counter-arguments (10)		
Accurate citation, quotation, etc. (5)		
Audience awareness (25)		
Consideration for different values (10)		
Appropriate tone (10)		
Correct genre for purpose (5)		
Grammar, spelling, punctuation (25 points)		
Clear sentence structure (10)		
Appropriate word choice (5)		
Correct spelling (5)		
Formatting requirements met (5)		
Final grade (out of 100):		

TECHNOLOGY IN THE WRITING CLASSROOM

Many of the teaching techniques outlined above adapt admirably to classroom technologies. Email, class Web sites, electronic drop boxes, blogs, MUDs and MOOs, word-processor commenting features, and other tools greatly increase your flexibility in assigning, collecting, and commenting on student work. These tools can enhance collaboration, enable the timely provision of feedback, and give students exposure to real audiences. Drop boxes let students turn in work at any time of the day or night. Commenting features allow you to comment on student papers electronically, so your comments are legible, correctly spelled, and intrude less upon the students' work. With email, you can quickly answer brief questions from students about their papers and send announcements and notices to the entire class. Message boards and forums can be used in many ways: by posting a topic and having students comment on it, or by having students post their class notes and observations, for example.

Since technological teaching tools vary so much from one institution to another, you will probably need to check with your own computer or technology office to determine what resources are available to you and your class. Whatever technologies you make use of in your classroom, there are a few common issues you should consider:

- Back up. This applies to you the instructor as much as to the students. Technology will inevitably fail, and often at the most critical moment. This means students should keep multiple copies of papers on disks and servers. It also means you should do the same with lesson plans and assignment sheets. Moreover, if you plan to use technology in class (say, an in-class Web search), it is always good to have a back-up plan for the day, just in case—one that doesn't rely on electricity.

- Tell students the first day of class how you will communicate with them. If you will be using an email list, have them write down their preferred email contact for you, and warn them that you expect them to check that address daily. If they miss an announcement, they will be held responsible. You should also tell them to expect a 24-hour response time on any email they send you. Otherwise, they may expect you to reply to their every query within minutes.

- Generally, it is best not to share with your students any personal Web pages such as MySpace, Facebook, etc. Students and teachers need some privacy from each other, which can be hard to accomplish in an online environment. Though your students may be comfortable with the entire world seeing the photos they post to Flickr, you will avoid a lot of problems if you keep these elements of their lives and yours separate.

- Remember that not all students have equal access to technology. While your school probably has a computer lab for all students, it may be crowded, hard for some students to get to, or simply not open at convenient times for all students. Students who don't have top-of-the-line technology at home shouldn't suffer in your class. Make sure the activities you assign are not placing an undue burden on any of your students.

Sample Syllabus for use with *Writing: A Guide for College and Beyond* Composition course with rhetorical focus

In a typical composition course, most instructors focus on four papers with significant time devoted to revising each one. Such a course will often cover the following aims:

Analyzing texts (chapter 10)

Analyzing causes (11)

Evaluating (12)

Arguing for a position (13) OR **Arguing for change** (14)

Usually, at least the final paper will have a research component. However, any and all of these papers could incorporate research. Here is a sample schedule you might use for a course of this nature:

Week	Focus	Assigned readings
1	Course introduction	Chapters 1, 2
2	Paper 1: Analysis of a text	Chapters 5,6, 10
3	Drafting techniques	Chapter 3; Return to Chapter 10 to review keys, *Staying on Track* issues
4	Revision	Chapter 4
5	Paper 2: Analyzing Causes	Chapter 11
6	Style workshop	Chapters 29, 30
7	Revision	Chapter 31; Return to Chapter 11 to review keys, *Staying on Track* issues
8	Paper 3: Evaluation (with visual component)	Chapter 12
9	Design considerations	Chapters 23, 24
10	Revision	Return to Chapter 12 to review keys, *Staying on Track* issues
11	Paper 4: Arguing for a position OR Arguing for change—research paper	Chapter 13 or 14; Chapter 15
12	Conducting research	Chapters 16-19
13	Drafting	Chapter 20
14	Citation	Chapter 21 or 22
15	Final revision	Review Chapter 20; Return to Chapter 13 or 14 to review keys, *Staying on Track* issues

Sample Syllabus for use with *Writing: A Guide for College and Beyond*
Writing course with a focus on technical, business, or science writing

In a course geared to students majoring in technical, business, or scientific fields, instructors often focus on the kinds of writing most common in those fields. Such a course might progress through the following aims:

Observing (Chapter 8)

Informing (Chapter 9)

Analyzing texts (Chapter 10)

Analyzing causes (Chapter 11)

Arguing for a position (Chapter 13)

At least the final two papers in a course like this would usually have a research component. Here is a schedule you might use for a course of this nature:

Week	Focus	Assigned readings
1	Course introduction	Chapters 1, 2
2	Observational essay assigned (a process, phenomenon, social activity, etc.)	Chapters 8, 3, and 4
3	Revision; observational writing assignment due	Chapters 29 and 30
4	Informative essay assigned (describing a theory, discovery, etc.)	Chapter 9
5	Research and revision	Chapters 15-19
6	Informative writing assignment due	Chapter 20
7	Analysis of a text assigned (analysis of a piece of disciplinary writing, such as an article, business plan, or report; students may also analyze graphs, charts, or other images rather than written texts)	Chapter 10
8	Visual design and analysis	Chapters 23 and 24
9	Analysis of a text due	Chapter 22
10	Group analysis of a cause assigned (why a particular software application crashes at given times; why a bank failed; why cholesterol builds up in arteries)	Chapter 11
11	Designing presentations	Chapters 27 and 28
12	Analysis of a cause due	no readings; in-class presentations
13	Argument for position assigned (which of two policies ought to adopted; which theory is most likely to adequately explain a phenomenon, etc.)	Chapter 13
14	Creating a work-world-ready report	Review Parts 4 and 5
15	Argument for a position due	

Sample Syllabus for use with *Writing: A Guide for College and Beyond*
Two-Semester Course

In a two-semester course, instructors and students have the luxury of exploring each of the aims outlined in *Writing: A Guide for College and Beyond*. Such an approach gives students a sustained experience with researching, drafting, and revising, in a wide variety of genres. Thus they get a clear picture of what each aim does differently, as well as the processes common to all writing projects. In this case, students can proceed fairly straightforwardly through the aims chapters as outlined in the chart below. (You might vary the times between assignments according to your school's holiday schedule and semester breaks—or simply to allow students more time on one paper or another.) In the weeks between assignments and due dates, students can conduct research, do in-class drafting and revision activities suggested in the text and in this manual, and conduct peer review:

Week 1: Course introduction

Week 2: Reflective essay assigned

Week 4: Refutation turned in; observation assigned

Week 7: Observational essay turned in; informative essay assigned

Week 10: Informative essay turned in; textual analysis assigned

Week 13: Textual analysis turned in; causal analysis assigned

Week 16: Causal analysis turned in; evaluation assigned

Week 19: Evaluation turned in; position argument assigned

Week 22: Position argument turned in; argument for change assigned

Week 25: Argument for change turned in; long research project assigned, built on 1-3 of preceding papers

Week 30: Research paper turned in

Students in a course like this will benefit even more if they keep a portfolio of their writing throughout the year. This portfolio can be reviewed several times during each semester, and turned in for assessment at the mid-point and end of the course.

Sample Syllabus for use with *Writing: A Guide for College and Beyond*
10-week Course

In a compressed session such as summer school, schedules for drafting and revision must be very carefully set. Readings must also be adjusted to meet the needs of particular classes without overwhelming students. You should plan to assign readings from Parts Four or Five of the text as needed to supplement the work students are doing on their papers.

In a composition course covering the basic rhetorical aims, papers on analysis, causation, evaluation, and proposal (with supporting research) could be scheduled as follows:

Week	Focus	Assigned readings
1	Course introduction	Chapters 1, 2
	Assign Paper 1: Analysis of a text	Chapters 5, 6, 10
2	Draft Paper 1, peer review	Chapter 3
	Revision workshop	Chapter 4
3	Paper 1 submitted; assign Paper 2: Analyzing Causes	Chapter 11
	Topic proposal review/drafting workshop	
4	Peer review of Paper 2	Chapters 29, 30, 31
	Revision and style workshop	
5	Final revision of Paper 2 submitted; assign Paper 3: Evaluation	Chapter 12
6	Targeted grammar revision and editing workshop	Part 5, as needed
7	Final revision of Paper 3 submitted; assign Paper 4: Arguing for change—research paper	Chapter 14
	Research overview; library tour	Chapter 15
8	Conducting research	Chapters 16-19
	Drafting workshop	Chapter 20
9	Peer review of Paper 4	
	Editing workshop	
10	Citation workshop	Chapter 21 or 22
	Final revision of Paper 4 due	

PART ONE: THE WRITER AS EXPLORER

Teaching recursive writing practices

These first four chapters introduce the concept of writing as a recursive process—one that involves multiple, repeated actions (exploring, thinking, drafting, revising)—rather than a start-to-finish task that happens in one sitting. Ideally, students will come to see in this section that writers need to circle back, returning to earlier ideas again and again. The ideas and activities in this section will set the tone for your course, and change students' perspectives about their writing. As college writers, they must see themselves going considerably above and beyond anything they have done previously in the writing classroom.

The first two chapters encourage students to re-see and re-think what they experience. Writers are human beings first, and their perceptions of the world around them are the basis of everything they write about. Then too, writers are readers—especially in college. *How* we read, as much as *what* we read, influences our thinking and writing.

Chapters 3 and 4 offer a way to dip into the writing process, previewing for your students how they will be expected to write in your course (and beyond!). They cover specific processes, such as drafting a thesis and responding to others' writing. A good plan is to preview them early in the semester, then return to them for guidance after students have received their first significant writing assignment—and for subsequent writing assignments as well.

Chapter One: Making Discoveries

> Be sure to access the resources available at *MyCompLab* go to
> (www.mycomplab.com and choose Faigley, *Writing: A Guide to College and Beyond*) to find additional writing exercises and tutorials.

Chapter goals: This chapter asks students to throw off their old preconceptions about writing and take a wider view. Prior to college, much of their writing has been about proving their proficiency as writers. In college, they will be expected to write in order to demonstrate the substance of their ideas. In order to have ideas, writers must have experiences, perceptions, and questions.

Chapter challenges: Some students may be happy to wander and explore, but have trouble harnessing that activity in the service of writing. Especially as you get to know your class early in the semester, it's probably a good idea to monitor the types of activities this chapter provides. Students may need to be reminded of their purpose for a particular task. They will also often need significant amounts of modeling to understand concepts like what makes a question "interesting."

Look with new eyes

Students have frequently been admonished to "write what they know," which isn't bad advice, but tends to limit them. This chapter pushes them to write from experience, but to make that experience fresh. They will be encouraged to explore, experience, act, notice, map, and question. They will have the opportunity to "unfocus" as they search for a topic. This helps break down the common stereotype of the good writer honing in on his or her topic with unerring precision, and shows student writers how to journey before they arrive.

Suggested in-class activity to introduce the chapter:

- Read the two-page opening spread of Chapter 1 in class.
- Send students outside *singly*—not in groups or pairs!
- Give them about 10 minutes to observe in the way the chapter describes. They might notice sounds, smells, sights, textures, artifacts, etc.
- When they come back, have them, *without talking*, spend three to four minutes writing a description, observation, or question about their outing.
- Allow them to refer to their writing (but don't require them to read it verbatim) while you discuss their experiences as a class.
- Pay attention to the varying degrees of fluency students exhibit with the assignment. For some, this kind of observation will be fairly easy. Others may find it harder.
- Ask students: How was this assignment different from most of your other writing assignments in the past? (They may note the experiential, spatial, or informal aspects of it.)
- Ask them: Is there anything you just did in fulfilling this assignment that you think you'd like to do again in the future? Did you learn anything that might influence your approach to future writing assignments? Students might answer these question out

loud, or in an informal sentence or paragraph for your review. Do not grade (except perhaps on a credit/no credit basis).

Explore the world

Moving outward from the directly personal and experiential, the text next invites students to consider signs and markers left by other human beings. Images and captions demonstrate how artifacts of others can spark questions, observations, and opportunities for exploration.

Write Now: **Discovering History**

Students can also do the assignment on page 5 at the oldest building on campus, in their dorms, or along shopping strips that feature campus bookstores and student hangouts. They can even try it in the classroom, if your room is fairly old—they might find history in obsolete audio-visual equipment, layers of paint, or even the graffiti on their desks. The key is for them to find history where it is unintentionally revealed—not, for example, by reading a photo display on The History of the Student Union.

Find a territory

The text next invites students to consider the possible directions that investigation can take. They are encouraged to focus on questions and think about what they hope to accomplish by writing. It is important for students to understand early that this kind of exploration—asking good questions, on topics that interest them—is not optional in college. They cannot expect to choose subjects that seem easy to write about and get good grades (or learn much). Make clear to your students that they can and should expect to contribute to existing knowledge in their college writing. It may not be easy, but it is what they are there for.

Learning Styles Focus
Write Now: **Mapping Your Campus**

The activity on page 7, using maps and brochures, is likely to appeal to strongly visual and spatial learners. Those who enjoy this activity might be encouraged to try Idea Mapping (see page 11) as they draft; they may also consider investigating visual and spatial topic areas (geography, architecture, fine arts, charting and graphing methodologies, etc.) for their papers.

This chapter's focus on informal writing and listing methods can do much to overcome students' general inertia when it comes to having ideas. Encourage them to try several of the techniques described: questioning, listing, taking inventory, brainstorming, nonstop writing, idea mapping, and subject searching. Try some as a class so everyone can see how multiple questions emerge from a single topic. Some methods may work better for some students than others. Remind your class that their preferred brainstorming method may change according to the reading, writing, and thinking they are trying to do at any given time.

Use guides

The chapter closes by suggesting to students that they use existing knowledge structures to spark their own ideas. Whether they know it or not, most students are already familiar with a number of guides (Google and Yahoo subject directories online, for example). As a class, try listing on the board all the guides they are familiar with (even *T.V. Guide*!). Discuss how each is organized and what it is used for (and who uses it). Ask: What features do most guides have in common? Why do you think they are different? If you have a networked classroom, you can take students on a brief tour of some guides in your library. Or, they can explore these options as a homework project.

Learning Styles Focus
Write Now: **Make an idea map**

Spatial learners can take the activity on page 11 one step further, putting each category and topic on a separate note card, and re-arranging the note cards as they work. They might group and re-group them, put them in sequential order, or stack them. This exercise gives writers a good sense of how simple it really is to re-arrange ideas.

You might conclude your study of this chapter by asking students to free-write briefly about how their conception of writing, or of writers, has changed since the class began.

Chapter Two: Reading to Explore

> Be sure to access the book specific resources available at *MyCompLab* go to
> (www.mycomplab.com and choose Faigley, *Writing: A Guide to College and
> Beyond*) to find additional readings and questions, as well as additional writing
> exercises and tutorials.

Chapter goals: This chapter seeks to show students the value of active reading. It
encourages the formation of what is not just a valuable *skill*, but a valuable habit as well.
Rather than reading passively or perhaps with a highlighter in hand, students should learn
to interrogate texts with specific questions and observations about them.

Chapter challenges: We learn to read at such an early age that sometimes we forget
what hard work it is. Depending on what and why they have read before reaching college,
students may or may not read deeply. If they have been bored by their prior reading, they
may have developed the habit of skimming for basic comprehension, to get to the end of
the piece as soon as possible. The sheer volume of reading required in college reinforces
this habit. Getting students interested in a piece of writing goes a long way toward
breaking the habit, but they may have to work on developing their self-discipline a bit as
well.

Developing active reading habits is crucial in college. This chapter walks students through a
number of active reading techniques. Practicing them in class and discussing them will help
students understand why active reading is so important.

Become a critical reader

After students have read through the questions in the box on page 13, provide a short writing
sample—an ad, editorial, news article, etc. As a class, go through the four sets of questions. You
might then wish to have them do the same with another piece of writing—perhaps one with a
very different source, bias, or purpose. Additionally, or alternatively, you can have them view an
image or object and use the questions on page 14.

After discussing the writing through the critical questions, ask students how much they learned
about the piece through questioning. What had they not noticed before that asking questions
helped them to see?

> *Write Now*: **Analyze information for students on your campus**
>
> Students can also do the activity at the bottom of page 13 using an ad,
> flyer, or promotional brochure they have collected on or around campus,
> or which they received in the mail, under their windshield wiper, etc.
> Such student-targeting items are usually easy to find at the beginning of a
> semester.

Look with a critical eye

From critical reading, the book moves on to critical *seeing*. We are confronted with sophisticated images on a daily basis—in advertisements, artwork, architecture, and entertainment. Yet little emphasis is placed on analyzing images the way we analyze texts. Visual analysis is also a good way for writers to stretch their vocabularies, as they hunt for words and phrases to describe what they are seeing. Precision and concreteness are almost always desirable traits in writing, and visual analysis hones these skills.

Working Together: **Analyze political cartoons**

Before beginning the activity on page 15, you may wish to have students briefly discuss their understanding of a "political cartoon." Is "Doonesbury" a political cartoon, for example? Why or why not?

You may also wish to have your students consider questions like, "How much text is in the cartoon? How would the cartoon's message change if the text were removed?"

Read actively

Annotation is a critical skill for college students. It vastly increases the amount of information they retain from their reading. You might show them a page or two from a book you have read and annotated, as an example. They should be gently discouraged from using highlighters as they read (though highlighters can be useful for organizing drafts of their *own* writing as they revise). Students should also, of course, be reminded not to write in library books.

This chapter offers numerous methods of annotating, and students should be encouraged to try several of them, to find what they are most comfortable with. You can do this with the entire class, using a single reading. To encourage students to interact with a text, you might provide a sample reading that is likely to irritate them (editorials about irresponsible youth are a reliable choice). Have students read a copy of the text and circle or mark in some way everything in the text that they disagree with. They can even map out the argument of the essay as described on the bottom of page 17. Encourage them to respond directly to the author if they wish, not just to the text. Stress that "anything goes," as long as it is an honest response.

Then, put a clean copy of the article overhead and ask students what portions they marked. Note where their responses converged on certain areas of the text. Ask them about their written comments (they do not have to read exactly what they wrote). Call special attention to comments that raise questions, offer evidence-backed refutation, or identify logical errors in the piece (this previews the section on formal logical fallacies that follows). This process allows all students to share in the experience of creating an enriching response to a single text.

In addition to the techniques described in the text (circling, finding major points, drawing lines and arrows to connect passages, asking questions, mapping, and making notes), here are a few more students can try:

- Put an X in the margin every time you see a word whose meaning you don't know. You can go back later and look it up.

- For each paragraph, write a single phrase or sentence in the margin summarizing that paragraph. If you read down the margins, you will have an outline summary of the entire piece.

- Underline what seems to be the main idea in each paragraph.

Additionally, ask students if they have other annotation strategies they use that they would like to share with the rest of the class.

Recognize fallacies

Now that students have some tools for critical reading under their belts, the text gives them specific advice that should be heeded whenever they read: Watch out for logical fallacies! If students can identify fallacies in their reading, they are less likely to use them in their writing. But logical fallacies are so common in everyday media like advertisements that we have almost come to expect them. Students may resist labeling either-or, hasty generalizations, or bandwagon claims as "bad writing."

If they are indifferent to identifying fallacies, you might make the case this way: Would you want a surgeon who was about to operate on you to make decisions based on hasty generalizations? "She says her stomach hurts; that's almost always appendicitis." Of course not. You want a doctor who will logically deduce, using all the available evidence, what is wrong with you. Logical fallacies may not hurt too much in some areas of our lives, such as what shoes we buy or how we rationalize eating one more slice of pizza than we really should. But in areas of human knowledge, health, and society, fallacies have no place. In college, where the advancement of human knowledge is a primary goal, there is a shared understanding that logic will carry the weight of argument. If fallacies appear in your college writing they will seriously weaken your credibility.

After reading through the list of fallacies, ask your students to come up with their own examples of the various types of fallacies. They might do this on their own, or you could assign groups to formulate examples of each category of fallacy. Ask them to try to think of examples they have actually seen or heard. This activity makes a nice lead-in to the Write Now activity at the bottom of page 19.

> ### *Write Now*: Analyze opinion writing
>
> Students can continue the activity on page 19 in many ways. You might have each student read and describe his or fallacy for the class. You could have students write a response to the author of the fallacy, explaining why it is illogical. Or, you could consider all the fallacies together and look for patterns among them: what is the most common fallacy identified? What samples or types of writing combined the greatest number of fallacies? How do the fallacies affect students' opinions of the writers?

Respond as a reader

Finally, this chapter encourages students to enter into a dialogue with their reading. This represents a step forward from simply responding in the margins of a work. College students must see themselves as participants in ongoing discussions, not spectators on the sidelines. Writing notes, summaries, and reading journals are all ways students can begin conceptualizing themselves as fellow scholars with ideas of their own.

Another method they can try is a dialogic response to a text. Dividing each sheet of paper into two columns, they should summarize or map (see page 17) the material in one column. In the other column, they comment on and question that material. This is an excellent method for retention of material as well as comprehension; suggest that they try this technique as they take class notes, as well.

> ### *Write Now*: Respond to what you read
>
> You may wish to suggest some ways students can "expand or extend" the reading they choose, such as recalling a similar experience (personal or anecdotal); thinking about the author's purpose or biases; disagreeing; asking questions (this could be a list rather than a paragraph); etc. If they get stuck, you can group students who chose the same piece (though this works better if you have already limited their choice to four or five different pieces).

You might conclude this chapter by having students list two or three annotating and responding techniques they plan to keep using.

Chapter Three: Planning a Journey

> Be sure to access the resources available at *MyCompLab* go to (www.mycomplab.com and choose Faigley, *Writing: A Guide to College and Beyond*) to find additional writing exercises and tutorials.

Chapter goals: This chapter shows students the large-scale structural possibilities available to them as writers. Ideally, a writer will visualize several organizational strategies as he or she composes, and select the best one for the particular purpose, audience, and aim of the writing.

Chapter challenges: There are so many purposes and formats for college writing that students may feel overwhelmed at first. But it's important that they understand their purpose before they start formulating a thesis; otherwise, they will often settle on an organizational strategy that does not make sense for their purpose. Students may be accustomed to writing with standard testing formats like the five-paragraph essay, which have little or no relation to purpose and audience. Taking responsibility for the direction and shape of their writing can be a daunting task, but it should be empowering as well.

Determine your direction

The dominant analogy in Chapter 3 is spatial—that good writing requires a "center." This should be a more friendly concept for students than the "thesis sentence" they have heard so much about, but which remains a mystery to many of them. The chapter also discusses the thesis as a "destination" toward which writers and readers journey. A key theme is the idea of bringing readers safely along on a journey (this theme is further developed in Part Two, The Writer as Guide), where neither the writer nor the audience gets lost or confused. Students and instructors alike should remember that destinations can change in mid-journey.

To introduce this chapter, you might have a class discussion about common routes and organizational plans on your campus. Why is there a trail worn in the grass between the student union and the gym? What do students consider the "center" of campus? How do they go about finding a specific room when they enter a building? Help students make the connections implied by the analogy; roughly:

direction of a journey = purpose of a writing task

a central organizing space = a thesis statement

a route = an organizational plan

Students may be a little puzzled by this analogy if they take it too literally. They may point out, for example, that buildings can be navigated in different ways but writing is typically read from start to finish. In this case, ask students how often they read a newspaper or their favorite magazine through from beginning to end. Are they more likely to skip around to certain parts? The reality is that much workplace writing isn't read from start to finish (this is why executive summaries are ubiquitous). This is a good opportunity to point out how different fields have different organizational patterns, which arise from the different ways documents are expected to be read.

An important point: the text notes that "the assignment will tell you which direction to go." As an instructor, ask yourself honestly if this is always true of the assignments you give your students. If it is not, you may want to build more direction into your writing assignments. You will probably find that it helps students immensely, and results in better papers.

The aims chapters of Part Two are previewed here; you can go through them all or you can focus on those you know your students will be writing during the course. Ask them if they have any ideas about which disciplines will typically use each aim. You might also ask which of these kinds of writing they have already done, and for what purposes.

Write a thesis

The examples of thesis statements in this section can help you check your students' understanding of "direction." Have them read each one, and then explain what language, exactly, in the thesis points it in the specific direction called for by the aim. For example, the "Argue" thesis makes the claim that laws "should" be passed—a clear indicator to readers that we will be reading an argument fleshing out this claim.

You can also duplicate this process as a class with another topic area, such as filesharing and intellectual property rights; vegetarianism, veganism, and organic foods; etc. Have students try to create a thesis about the topic that heads in each of the seven directions. But stress that this is an exercise in formulating different kinds of theses as *starting points* for building a paper. A working thesis may change a lot before the paper is finally finished.

The advice in "Evaluate your working thesis" will be more useful to students once they are working on a specific assignment, so plan on having them come back to this section when they are at that stage. However, you can have them try it now with one of the sample theses they have created for the preceding activity. But don't go overboard. It's probably best not to have them invest a lot of energy in polishing a thesis that's not going to be used in a paper.

Write Now: **Write a bold thesis**

The activity on page 25 is intended to stretch students' conceptions of what makes a good argument. The theses they come up with therefore may not seem especially plausible as arguments. After they have written their paragraphs, discuss the pluses and minuses of a bold thesis. It may be more difficult to argue for and require more effort to find supporting evidence, but it usually makes a far more interesting piece of writing.

Plan your route

Continuing the analogy of journey, the chapter now asks students to consider different ways of reaching the destination set out by their theses. This is another good time to remind them that destinations can change a bit as a journey progresses. In fact, it is difficult to fully realize a thesis statement without doing some planning and drafting.

Learning Styles Focus
Determine a plan

Like the Write Now activity on page 11, the exercise on page 26 is excellent for visual and spatial learners. If you use sticky notes, you could have students arrange their topics in different sections of the classroom walls. Then everyone can mingle, looking at their peers' organizational strategies. If they like, they can use additional sticky notes to leave comments for one another.

Strongly aural learners may wish to use a voice recorder to read through all their notes and describe an organizational plan verbally. They can then go back and listen to the recording, writing or typing out the plan as they recorded it.

Making a writing plan, or translating a spatial map into a more linear outline, is a tricky step. Students should be encouraged (as in the Write Now activity at the bottom of page 27) to try more than one arrangement of their outline. If you plan to have them turn in a formal outline, ask them to start with a working outline, which you can look over and make suggestions about. Again, this activity will seem more purposeful, and less like busy work, if students try it once they have embarked on a full-length writing assignment.

Write Now: **Make a plan**

Have students save the writing plan they create from this activity. After their paper is finished, ask them to go back to it and notice how the finished paper adheres to or departs from the plan. What unforeseen developments changed their plan? What elements of the paper went exactly as planned?

You might conclude your study of this chapter by having students write briefly about the aims (or "directions") described here that they are most interested in trying to explore as writers.

Chapter Four: Returning and Revising

Be sure to access the resources available at *MyCompLab* go to (www.mycomplab.com and choose Faigley, *Writing: A Guide to College and Beyond*) to find additional writing exercises and tutorials.

Chapter goals: This chapter stresses the need to defer closure on a piece of text until it has taken its best possible form. Revising (changing large-scale features of a piece of writing) and editing (small-scale changes like correcting punctuation) should be seen by students as two distinct acts, with very different purposes. This chapter also demonstrates for student writers the kind of specific questions that will help them and their peers revise.

Chapter challenges: Inexperienced writers (and those who, perhaps because of unpleasant past experiences, find writing difficult) will often resist the necessary suspension of closure that experienced writers practice as a matter of course. They will instead want to finish a piece of writing as soon as possible—settling on a thesis that is "probably good enough," writing straight through their rough draft, knocking out one paragraph per outline item, and tacking on a simplistic or redundant conclusion. Then they will "revise" by correcting whatever surface features they notice are problematic. The fact is that going back into one's hard-won writing and making drastic changes to it is a daunting task, and one that many writers will avoid if at all possible. But "re-seeing" your work through a reader's eyes is critical if a draft is to change from a record of the writer talking to himself or herself to an attempt to truly communicate with others.

See again

The chapter opens by describing what happens when we come back to a familiar place after time away. The concept of looking back over writing is very important, but just as important, and far less often emphasized, is the need to leave it first. As the song says, "How can I miss you if you won't go away?" This is one reason it's so important to build time into each paper assignment. It isn't all time for students to be working. Some of it is time for them to be doing other things, so that they can return to their writing with a fresh perspective before revising.

Of course, some of your students will persist in writing their papers in one burst of effort the night before it is due. But give all of them the opportunity, at least. Many of them *will* take you up on it, and they will learn a valuable skill in doing so.

To introduce this chapter, consider having students free-write for a moment or two about an experience they have had like the one outlined at the top on page 28. Perhaps they went back to visit their elementary school, or returned to a town where they used to live. What seemed different to them about the place? What had changed about the place? How had they themselves changed while they were away? Discuss their responses as a class. Talk about the fact that we see ourselves in relation to our surroundings—and our writing. Since we are changing every minute of our lives, it stands to reason that time away from a place, or a draft, brings us back to it a different person, with more experience and a different perspective.

The activity described on page 28 will be especially helpful to those who learn best by hearing new information. However, this is a wonderful opportunity to show all your students how different methods can reinforce their learning. Reading one's own paper aloud, or hearing another person read it to you, is unquestionably one of the best ways for writers to "see" problems in the text. Hearing errors read aloud somehow makes them more "visible."

You might also have your students look back at something they wrote, even informally, a class or two ago—this could be something you collected and hand back to them now (or, if they have papers from earlier semesters, those would be good too). Ask them: Would they change anything about their writing today? What? Why? (Don't, however, do this activity with newly-graded papers; students will simply say they would change whatever you had noted they should change.)

Evaluate your draft

Have students bookmark this page so they can refer back to it during each writing project. If you initially go over this chart without an assignment already in process, focus on the left-hand column, showing students the broad categories of questions they should be concerned with. Hopefully, these issues will be addressed in your grading criteria for any assignment (see the section on Evaluating Student Writing in the earlier part of this manual for more information on grading criteria).

With your students, look at the list of strategies on page 30. Ask them:

- Which ones have they used before when they revise?

- Which do they use most often?

- Are there any they *never* use? Why not?

- After they have had one paper graded, you can ask: "Are there any you didn't use but wish you had?"

Hearing their peers talk about successful ways to employ these techniques may help students decide they are worth trying.

Respond to others

Having covered self-review of work, the text now moves on to peer review. Broadening the circle of people who read and respond to drafts dramatically increases the writer's ability to revise effectively. However, peers must respond effectively in order to be helpful to the writer. Think of this table as a bare-bones set of direction for peer review (see the section on Peer

Review earlier in this manual for more information on peer review, and sample directions and handouts). Ideally, you will key peer review instructions to a particular assignment. But this chart gives students a good overview of the process, and explains what they need to keep in mind as they read and respond.

Pay attention to details last

Finally, the text turns our attention to the issue that most students want to address first: editing. This is not to say that students shouldn't fix errors as they find them. But they shouldn't focus on hunting for errors before they have revised their paper on a larger scale. For one thing, correcting errors invests a great deal of energy in a draft, making students less inclined to change it in any major way. Students will not want to "un-do" all their work, make large-scale changes, and then be faced with the task of correcting errors all over again.

As on page 30, ask students which of the strategies on page 32 they already use on a regular basis. Which ones do they think they need to focus on most to improve their own drafts? Which of them do they need the most help with or get the most frustrated about? For specific attention to improving writing style, see Part Five of the textbook.

Write Now: **Analysis of an ad**

Have students try the activity on page 32 alone, and then move them into groups to compare their responses. Did they find the same kinds of strengths and weaknesses? Were some problems more troublesome than others? Does everyone agree on the ways the essay could be improved?

After they have discussed the substantive problems with the draft, you can let students find grammatical and mechanical errors in the paper (some will have a strong urge to do so). Rather than immediately correcting these, ask students instead to articulate what about the error is confusing or misleading. Why is it a problem for readers?

You could conclude your class's study of this chapter by using the two lists of revision and editing strategies to prompt student reflection on their revision process. Have them write two short letters to you, one submitted with their rough draft (using the list on page 30) and one with the final draft (referring to the list on page 32). Ask them to briefly tell you which strategies they used in revising, and which types of changes they need help with. These letters will help you direct your feedback to the areas the students are most concerned about.

PART TWO: THE WRITER AS GUIDE

Teaching the Aims Chapters

This section of *Writing: A Guide for College and Beyond* introduces students to the crucial concept that writing in college is done for different purposes and different audiences—that it has different aims. Chapters 7 through 14 each introduce one specific aim.

To reinforce the message of the aims chapters, encourage your students to talk about the writing they are doing (or reading) for their other classes, and what aims they cover. Discuss the audience and purpose for each. This is a good way to overcome the challenges outlined below for Chapters 5 and 6: students' desire to adapt old, unsatisfactory forms to college writing purposes, and their lack of experience with the varied audiences of college writing.

The aims chapters begin by describing the type of writing under consideration, and the purposes it is used for. Students are given methods to find a topic for a given aim, audience considerations, and other specific directions for fulfilling that aim. Each chapter also describes "keys" to successfully fulfilling its aim. An annotated example of each aim follows; the annotations highlighting where directions and keys are employed by the author. Use the annotated example to show students how the keys are employed in the "real world." Seeing key features of an aim as they function in another writer's work will prepare them to look for these features in their peers' work, in other work that they read, and in their own writing. Note that the annotated reading shows only one way to employ the keys—students should be reminded that the keys can be employed in many ways. This fact is then demonstrated in the un-annotated examples that follow.

The "How to Read . . ." feature preceding these examples primes students to actively read and think about the variety of writing represented. For each sample, Analyzing and Connecting questions guide students through an investigation of the piece's aim and means of achieving it. In this way, students can get a sense of the breadth of each aim: how it might be put to different purposes, for different audiences, with different effects. Use these readings to help students avoid a "fill in the blanks" approach to the aim. After reading some examples of a genre, students will be less likely to simply follow guidelines without really considering their purpose. And there are a wide variety of sample essays (in addition to the annotated example), so there is certain to be some topic or approach that will appeal to every student, giving each a reason to investigate the aim through reading. In the section that follows, this manual provides advice on assigning and discussing the readings for Chapters 7 through 14. We also provide a detailed description of how to use readings to introduce Chapter 8.

Next, each chapter takes students on a step-by-step journey to writing with the aim it has described. As students prepare to write their own document and achieve the aim, they will want to refer to the two-page process chart in the chapter. These charts graphically depict and describe the writing process in terms tailored to each aim. Each step is then broken down on the pages that follow, with detailed direction and advice, paired with a sample of student writing demonstrating each step of the process. Students will benefit from seeing how "incomplete" some stages look. The whole provides an overview of how a paper with this aim might realistically come together over time— not always smoothly or neatly, but effectively in the end.

The Staying on Track feature that appears throughout the aims chapters serves the vital function of warning students about common mistakes to avoid. Direct students' attention to these boxes before and as they draft and revise, to head off problems before they happen. These boxes can also be used to help guide students through peer review; you might incorporate the points in them into any peer review worksheets or handouts you give your students. The points in Staying on Track will also help you prioritize comments on rough drafts; consider using them to draw up comment sheets (see the section on Working with Student Writing earlier in this manual).

Note that, although research is covered in Part Three of *Writing: A Guide for College and Beyond*, virtually all of the aims in Part Two can involve research. As you read through the samples in these chapters, point out to students places where the authors rely on outside sources to make their points. And as you design assignments for these chapters, think about where you can incorporate research, so students get as much experience as possible with this critical college and life skill.

Chapters 7 through 14 each end with a number of projects students might undertake as they explore the chapter aim. You can use or adapt these projects for your own class, even expanding them into full-length papers if you like. We've provided full-fledged assignment sheets for each project in Chapter 7, and suggestions in each succeeding chapter on how to assign each project, and support students may need as they complete it.

Chapter Five: Writing in College

> Be sure to access the resources available at **MyCompLab** (www.mycomplab.com) and choose Faigley: *Writing: A Guide to College and Beyond* to find additional support and writing exercises.

Chapter goals: This chapter seeks to help students understand that some elements are common to *all* college writing, but that others depend on your purpose, or aim, and your audience.

Chapter challenges: Though they may understand the concepts in this chapter theoretically, students often resist enacting them in their writing. They may have grown comfortable with the standard aims and corresponding forms often taught prior to college: the five-paragraph essay, the personal opinion essay, or the literature summary. Rather than assess new audiences and purposes, they often attempt to force college writing tasks into these unsatisfactory structures. It's important to help them see how powerful the new aims are for learning and communicating college-level ideas—and how ill-suited the old forms are.

You could introduce this chapter by asking about the range of writing that students have already done. Many will tell you they have written research papers and essays, but you may be surprised at the breadth of some of their experience. In high school did they write for any classes outside of English? Which ones? What kinds of documents did they produce? Whatever their experience, stress that they are likely to do more writing, in a greater variety of classes, now that they are in college.

Understand the demands of writing in college
The chapter begins by referring to the very broad range of college writing demands. Students may have an idea of the range of courses they will take in college, but they probably don't yet appreciate what a wide range of adjustments they will have to make in their writing from discipline to discipline. Frequently, they think that writing is writing, period. What they need to understand is that writing involves thinking, and that the kinds of thinking they employ will now have to vary from assignment to assignment. Go over the critical thinking skills required for the expectations in the chart on page 37.

Think about your aim
Here the concept of "direction" introduced in Part One is fully fleshed out into purpose-driven genres. Ask students to think of arguments or topics they have read that demonstrate the various aims in the chart on page 05/04 (not necessarily for school):

- What evaluations have they written or read (movie reviews, Amazon.com book reviews)?

- Have they done any reflective writing out of school (diary, journal, blog)?

- Did they use any of these aims in the essay they wrote for college admission (if they wrote one)?

- Have they read an autobiography, Anne Frank's diary, or some other reflective work? They can jot down a list to refer to during discussion, or just volunteer their responses aloud.

Working Together: **Using aims to create thesis statements**

As with similar activities in Part One, you should remind students that what they are manipulating in the activity on page 39 are *working* topic sentences—beginning efforts to get writers started toward their goal. Polishing a thesis before any research or drafting has taken place is often counter-productive (and rarely the way writers really work), so make sure students see these examples in the larger context. You could also come up with a list of subjects as a class, then work in groups, come back together, and compare each group's theses. How do different people find different ways of looking at the same subject?

Think about your genre

Genre is often assigned in college, rather than being a matter of pure choice. The same is largely true in the work world. Encourage students to think actively about other genres they already write in: text messages, email, notes to professors, letters to parents, etc. Most are probably informal. Ask in particular about any on-the-job writing they have already done. Note that any genre, even an informal one, can provide useful information. But not all readers will read all genres. If you owed a friend a letter and sent him a 30-page report on everything you had done in the last month, would he read it? Would you text-message your boss to explain why you missed an important meeting? So *choosing* the best genre is important when it isn't assigned. When genre *is* assigned, students should think carefully about, and ask questions about, how the genre matches its audience. Instructors (particularly in the disciplines) often assume this is obvious to students, but that is not in fact true.

Write Now: **Compare styles across genres**

As they do the activity on the bottom of page 41, you can also encourage your students to look for differences in *content* and *persuasiveness* among the genres they have found. Do some genres seem inherently more convincing than others? Why? Do some include content that others leave out?

One way you can conclude this chapter is to ask students to log, for 24 hours or until the next class, the genre of everything they read. Being on the lookout for different genres will help them learn each one's distinguishing features. This gives you a chance to remind them of the difference between genre and medium. Articles in a newspaper, for example, may have informative, expressive, or persuasive aims.

This may also help students see how little experience they have with *academic* genres, since most of their reading is probably outside of academia. And when they report back to class with their lists, you may find some who aren't sure what genre a piece of writing falls into. As a class, see if you can fit these oddities into a category—or if you need to create a new one.

Chapter Six: Writing Effectively

Be sure to access the resources available at *MyCompLab* (www.mycomplab.com) and choose Faigley: *Writing: A Guide to College and Beyond* to find additional support and writing exercises.

Chapter goals: This chapter introduces students to the concept of the audience at the college level: various groups with different levels of expertise, with definite expectations. It seeks to show students the importance of establishing their own credibility as they address an audience.

Chapter challenges: Prior to college, students will usually have experience with only a few, mostly predictable, audiences: their teacher, with whom they have a direct if formal relationship, whatever friends and family they write to, and the impersonal audience of standardized test graders who have rated their most heavily-emphasized writing. None of these audiences really represents the audiences students will write for in college. While students will write for their instructors, those instructors will often be specialists in a given field, looking for explicit disciplinary aspects of the writing they grade. It may take a while before college audiences begin to seem "real" to your students.

There are many ways to get students to think about audience. As you begin this chapter, focus on how students see themselves, and how they want others to see them. You might give them a list of character traits, such as:

trustworthy
devious
intelligent
friendly
unhelpful
knowledgeable
angry

Ask them which they would want readers to associate with them (they don't have to volunteer their preferences out loud!). Next, ask them if they have ever thought about writers having these traits. Have they ever read something and felt the writer was lying to them? Have they read something they felt sounded especially authoritative? Ask for examples of writing that personifies certain traits. Discuss the specific attributes of the writing that give these impressions about the writer.

Understand the rhetorical situation

The chapter begins by introducing the classical rhetorical triangle—a simple and effective model for thinking about almost any kind of writing situation. In addition to the example given in the text, you might run through a few more to show students how the writer-audience-text triangle is formed: an editorial in the paper by a well-known diplomat will carry a certain ethos because of the writer's experience and importance. She will probably make a number of points about the likely causes and possible solutions for a problem, such as a famine somewhere in the world (logos). She may use pathos to appeal to the reader's emotions by describing the terrible suffering being endured in the famine-stricken region.

Ask students which types of appeals they personally respond to most often. What kinds do they usually ignore, and why? Which kinds of appeals are most likely to evoke a negative reaction (think about commercials that annoy you)? Which kinds of appeals would you use in the following situations?

- Asking a friend to lend you money.

- Telling your parents about an accident you had with their car.

- Explaining to a younger sibling how to apply to a college.

- Asking a teacher for an extension of a due date.

Think about your audience

The text next points out something that seems obvious but often hasn't occurred to students before: not having a face-to-face audience makes writing very, very different from most of the other communicating we do. It makes it harder to gauge the appropriate tone. It makes the selection and arrangement of ideas doubly important, because there is not opportunity to adjust based on audience response (confused looks, questions). One reason college writing is so difficult for students is that they are now encountering audiences they know next to nothing about, and can only guess at their expectations. To compensate, students need to actively learn as much as they can about their audience, and then use their imaginations and common sense to fill in the rest of the blanks. They will need considerable help from you to do this successfully—especially in the beginning.

Note that when the text says "Good college writing involves an element of surprise," the term refers to the sense of discovery, of mystery-solving, that is the heart of college writing. Make certain students don't misinterpret this as a license to engage in non sequiturs (see the section on fallacies in Chapter 2) throughout their writing.

Working Together: Analyzing Advertisements

As they do the activity on page 44, students can also compare advertisements in each magazine with editorial content. Do the ads and articles contradict at all in terms of audience? For example, women's magazines may have lots of recipes for high-calorie foods and ads for diet products. Men's magazines may have articles about confident, successful athletes, but feature ads for products to stop hair loss. What do these competing audience appeals tell you about the audience as a whole? Do these contrasts give you a more complex picture of the magazine's audience?

In a networked classroom, you could do this exercise on commercial

---

Web sites, looking at online content and advertising. Students may wish to consider a "smart" ad generator like Google ads, which appear on many sites and blogs. How well do these programs match the products they advertise with the presumed audiences of various Web sites?

Staying on Track: Know what college readers expect

The chart on page 45 is an excellent tool for students to keep handy as they draft their papers. Suggest that they bookmark it for future reference. As with the other *Staying on Track* boxes in this part of the book, these concepts listed here will probably be useful to you when you are devising peer review and commenting on rough drafts.

Ask your students which of the expectations listed here they usually find easiest to meet. Which is the hardest for them? Why? What might they do to make certain they meet this expectation in future papers?

Think about your credibility

If you opened your study of this chapter with the character traits activity suggested above, you can now refer back to it. Of course, while everyone would *like* to be considered concerned, well-informed, fair, and ethical, communicating these qualities in writing isn't always easy. Students should understand that good intentions aren't enough. They can *be* a very good person and still not reflect their good qualities in their writing. Specific textual attributes are needed for a piece of writing to communicate credibility.

Ask students to bring in examples of writing that does not strike them as credible. Share these examples and then discuss them in terms of the four qualities on page 46 (if your students take a while to warm up to discussion, have them think for a minute and write something on a note card before sharing). Which qualities did the writer neglect? Have students pinpoint specific places in examples of non-credible writing where these problems are evident. Also have them point out exact words and phrases that do communicate concern, fairness, etc.

Staying on Track: Build your credibility
After they have read the box on page 46, ask students to consider how a reader *feels* when reading each example. Do any words like the following come up?

- confused

- angry

- doubtful

- bored

65

Point out that such common emotional responses from readers can greatly diminish a reader's willingness to be persuaded—or indeed even to finish reading a piece of writing.

Become an effective writer

The chapter closes by summing up all the elements required in a college writing project. Here, students get a glimpse of the kind of final product they will be expected to produce in your class and in others. Ask students to assess their own abilities according to the list on page 48. What do they do well? What do they have trouble with? How can they improve the skills they feel are currently weak? Should they start assignments earlier, consult a handbook for grammar problems, or work on developing their vocabulary? Which criterion would they most like to see improve in their own writing? This might make an appropriate topic for a journal entry, or students can write a paragraph or two.

Sample essay: Angela Yamashita, *Got Roddick?*

This sample essay by student writer Angela Yamashita gives students a first look at all the many things they can get right in their papers. Point out such simple attributes as providing a title, captioning visuals, and citing sources.

To make this exercise even more effective, try it with a piece of student writing your own class can identify closely with. Give them a sample essay, or several, from past students who have given you permission (remove their names, of course). Have your class assess the qualities of effective writing. If you have an assignment sheet and grading criteria for the paper, distribute that as well. Help your students tie their assessment to specific attributes of the text, as the arrows do in the example on pages 49-51. They may start out with general observations about the essay's quality, but lead them back to the elements of the text that inform their judgment.

Chapter Seven: Reflecting

Be sure to access the resources available at **MyCompLab** go to
(www.mycomplab.com and choose Faigley, *Writing: A Guide to College and Beyond*). Book specific features include:
* Additional "Analyzing and Connecting" questions for every reading provide a wealth of class discussion and assignment options.
* Links to bonus readings you and your students can access on the Web along with "Analyzing and Connecting" questions provide a truly wide variety of reading assignment choices.
* Downloadable worksheets that support and extend the "How to Write" process maps provide helpful reinforcement.
* Additional "Write Now," "Staying on Track," and "Working Together" activities ensure students have varied and plentiful practice activities.
*   Additional Projects (major writing assignments) provide a rich source of additional assignments.

Chapter goals: This chapter seeks to move students away from reflection as a cursory activity and help them see it as a process that can lead to deeper, more complex understanding of the world and the individual. They should see that reflecting is not an entirely internal process. On the contrary, writing a good reflection takes consideration of audience and purpose.

Chapter challenges: Starting with reflective writing helps students by letting them focus on a topic about which they usually have excellent fluency: themselves. However, the temptation to naval-gaze and/or produce trite essays will be strong for some students. They may need to be pushed to take this kind of personal discovery to a level befitting college writing. The many excellent sample writings in the chapter will help them see what reflective writers can achieve, and what they should aspire to themselves.

You might begin this chapter by asking students to free-write for a few minutes on how their life has changed since they started college. What aspects of their lives do they enjoy more now, and which less? Which everyday tasks are easier, and which are harder? How has college changed them?

Discuss their thoughts as a class, letting each student volunteer ideas from his or her free-writing. What does this kind of reflection show them about themselves? What does it help them understand about their classmates?

Writing reflections

Reflection is different from simply remembering. Students may have some idea of what it means to reflect, but they have likely encountered this task in writing assignments that encouraged, or at least did not discourage, pat or even cliched responses (reflection being especially popular in essay testing). Ask them about their experiences with reflective writing—you will probably hear memories of in-class essay writing, etc.

Fortunately, students often feel as dissatisfied with these types of writing as do college instructors. Ask them what they liked or disliked about these assignments, and you may get an earful. Point out that in college, the kind of reflection they have done before is only a starting point. Hopefully, it will grow into something much more interesting to the reader, and valuable to the writer.

Students will want to return to the "components" and "keys" described on pages 54-55 as they begin their assignment. These are the critical elements that make a reflection what it is—and make a good reflection good, as well. If they follow the list of components, students are likely to generate a draft that meets their reflective assignment's basic requirements. If they follow the keys, they will stand a good chance of engaging readers effectively.

Ask your students how they themselves respond to the features described in Keys to Reflection when they read. Do they prefer honesty? Are they more likely to read on if an interesting story is being told? Explain that making their writing good often means writing the kinds of things they would like to read—a kind of Golden Rule for writers.

Working Together

Another possible strategy for the activity on page 55 is to have students look through their images in small groups. If no photos are available, they could even choose a selection of small objects from their purse or backpack. The point is for them to consider the *associative* qualities of the image or object. Not "What makes it cool?" or "What does it look like?" but "What else does it make me think of? What does it remind me of?"

An effective reflection

This essay is a deeply emotional memorial, but it provides much more information to the reader than simply an account of the author's feelings. In fact, the author's emotions are not really the focus of this reflection at all. After they have read the essay, ask students what they learned that they didn't know before. About history? About the author and her attitudes, beliefs, feelings? About her brother? You might list all the factual information the essay offers on the board or an overhead. Then ask about the other things the essay does. What makes this piece different from, say, a biography of Tet's life, or a newspaper obituary about him? Push your students to identify specific textual elements that make this piece a reflective essay (The curling incense smoke made hazy halos of the young faces who came mourning a dead friend," for example). You can refer to the keys on page 55 if you need to.

Assigning and discussing the readings

There are many ways to support student learning using the readings in this chapter. You might assign one for students to read before they come to class on the day you introduce the chapter. Or, if you aren't sure which reading will be most appealing to your students, allow them to choose one of the readings themselves (they are more likely to really understand the aim if they experience it in an essay they want to read).

Either way, by exposing students to the writing aim beforehand, you set your class up to discuss reflective writing in concrete, rather than abstract, terms. Once they have read an exemplary reflection, they will have a better sense of what reflective writing really is, and the description on pages 54-55 will have more resonance for them.

The How to Read Reflections questions in the box on page 60 will help students think about the context and background of a piece—why it was written, and how and by whom it was intended to be read. You should consider previewing these questions as a class.

You can make further use of the How to Read Reflections questions on page 60 if you think your students need more practice identifying the purpose and nature of reflective writing. Assign some or all of the questions for students to answer after they read one or two more sample essays. Don't overdo this, though. There is no need to pin down every element of every piece, and students shouldn't be led to believe that a good piece of reflective writing results from simply checking things off a list.

The Analyzing and Connecting questions preceding each writing sample are another nice preview feature. Students can read these questions before they read the sample, and then think about the points they raise as they read. Students might write up informal responses to the Analyzing and Connecting questions for a reading, and then refer to their responses during a classroom discussion of the reading. Or, you can use them to spark group discussions or free-writing or journal entries about the reading. Students can answer the questions in pairs or small groups, and then discuss their answers as a class. You can also make these responses more formal, and have students submit them for a homework grade.

Use the Components and Keys on pages 54-55 to talk about the readings. Can students identify concrete details in the readings? What organizational patterns do they notice? What is the focus of the reflection? By looking for attributes of good reflective writing, students begin to think about how they might build those attributes into their own writing.

In addition to looking for qualities that define good reflective writing, students should be on the lookout for qualities that make good writing, period. As they progress through the aims chapters, they will begin to notice common qualities of good writing across genres (clarity, detail, varied sentence structure, etc.).

Additional questions for discussion of the reflection samples:

- If you had written this essay or story, what one thing about it would you change?

- Do any parts of the reading not seem to fit the Keys and Components on pages 54-55? Why do you think the author did not follow those conventions for this aim?

- Which reading did you enjoy the most, and why?

- Which reading did you enjoy the least, and why?

What questions do your students come up with on their own about the writing samples?

Yet another way to use the writing samples is to have students read a pair of essays, and compare and contrast them in writing or in class discussion. They might write a brief comparison, or read the essays in advance and then generate lists of similarities and differences, as a class. Some good pairs for discussion in this chapter are:

- David Sedaris' *Let it Snow* and Pam Houston's *A Blizzard Under Blue Sky*—What is the challenge or conflict in each story? How does the weather shape the action? What similarities do students see in the themes of the two stories?

- Bharati Mukherjee's *Two Ways to Belong in America* and Amy Tan's *Mother Tongue*—
What is the purpose of each author in writing her reflection? What common experiences
do they share? In what ways do their responses differ?

If you have time, you could also ask students to read several, or all, of the readings, and discuss
the different ways they fulfill the keys and components of the genre. This will give students a
sense of the many options available in a genre, rather than focusing their attention on the
limitations and restrictions of the genre.

Finally, consider using the sample readings to help students assess their own understanding of
the aim. To do this, have students read one sample at the beginning of the unit, a second after
they submit rough drafts, and a third when they have submitted their final drafts. Discuss the first
reading in one or more of the ways described above. After the rough draft, have students read
another sample, and ask them to respond to questions such as: "Does this reading give you any
ideas for improving your draft?" "Does this writer use any techniques you are already using in
your paper?" "If you were reviewing this reading as a peer, what advice would you give the
writer?" After the final draft, ask students to read and respond to a third sample, considering such
questions as "How does this writer's tone differ from the tone I used in my essay?" and "Does
this author use more or less detail than I did in my essay?"

How to write a reflection
The chart on pages 90-91 gives students an overview of the process they will generally follow
when writing a reflection. Make sure they understand, though, that charts are deceptively simple,
and this one doesn't literally depict the way writers really work. Still, this chart breaks down in
an easy-to-read form the many tasks students are likely to need to focus on at given stages of
their project. The chart also serves as a good reminder when they are first thinking about their
assignment: there are many steps to go through, and they shouldn't wait until the last minute to
start.

1. Find a reflective topic and a focus for writing about it
The best way to get your class off to a good start on a reflective writing assignment is to make
certain they are all responding actively to their chosen object for reflection, with curiosity and
focused attention. If that is the case, all other obstacles you meet can be overcome. If a student
doesn't seem genuinely excited about a topic, encourage him or her to keep searching, and to talk
to classmates for ideas.

If students have trouble finding a focus, try having them think about it as an "approach" or a
"treatment," or even a "hook." Whatever they have chosen to write about can be looked at in a
completely mundane way. Ask them to describe the "regular" way of seeing their object. Then
challenge them to explain how their way of looking at the object differs. That shift from obvious
to something different is their focus.

71

2. Develop a response

Here is where students can really benefit from losing their inhibitions. At this stage in their writing process, they should feel free to write down any and every idea that occurs to them. The more ideas they generate now, the more they will have to choose from when they begin to write a draft. So encourage lots of writing at this stage—some of it in class, if possible. When they have several times more material than they think they will need for their paper, students can begin to organize what they have, selecting the best ideas, and organizing them according to the focus that has hopefully emerged.

3. Write a draft

If students have generated a lot of details and ideas, this part of the writing process will likely be messy but not too fraught emotionally. If, however, they do not have enough material to work with, they will struggle at this point. Students who do not really have enough content to fulfill the assignment should not waste time worrying about tone and their choice of title. Send them back to the generative stage, with brainstorming, more observation, or a visit to the writing center. Try not to let them change subjects at this point—usually, students will experience the same mental block with the new subject, and be twice as far behind.

Writer at Work: Outlining

In order to produce a working outline like this one, student writer Janine Carter probably had to do a considerable amount of writing first. She obviously already had a rough idea of which topics would support a full paragraph or more.

Have students refer back to the assignment sheet Carter is working from. What elements of her outline fulfill which requirements of the assignment? Make sure they are keeping their own assignment particulars in mind as they draft their essays.

---

4. Revise, revise, revise

This section of the text covers the work of large-scale revision and that of small-scale editing, but never let your students forget the difference! The first five categories—meeting the assignment, focusing the subject, adding detail, considering tone, and organizing effectively— are by far the most important.

Writer at Work: Introduction and conclusion

Notice that student writer Janine Carter has focused on elements of her introduction and conclusion that she considers mundane or "boring." They were perfectly good concepts to use while drafting her paper, and they make sense. But they are not very inspiring and tweaking them helps the introduction and the conclusion do justice to the rest of the essay. Have students compare the paragraphs on page 101 with the beginning and end of the final version of the essay, on pages 102-105. Was there anything "wrong" with the phrases Carter marked on the rough drafts? Do your students agree that her changes were made for the better? Why or why not?

---

5. Student essay

This finished essay gives your students a chance to look for the keys to reflective writing in a non-professional piece of work. You might, as a class or individually, annotate this essay like the Embrey essay at the beginning of this chapter.

Projects

For this chapter, we have provided below three full assignment sheets drawn from the projects on pages 106-107. For chapters 8-14, we provide suggestions that you can use in conjunction with these models to create assignments from all the projects in this section. Each assignment here includes a "platforming" activity, breaking out one of the key writing tasks into a separate assignment. These assignments also provide a timetable for drafting and revision of the paper, criteria for their evaluation, and references to sections of the textbook students will want to refer back to as they work.

Assignment: Reflection on the Past

Based on *Writing: A Guide for College and Beyond*, page 106

Write a 3-5-page essay about a person, place, or event in your past that has special significance.

Using the concepts covered in Chapter 7 of the text, you will write a reflective essay about a person, place, or event in your past. You should think of your audience as being people who do not know you at all. Do *not* assume your audience has a lot in common with you (age, interests, economic status). You should try to find a way to make your reflection interesting to a wide array of readers.

Following the steps outlined on page 106 of the text, you will choose and focus your topic, and write a topic proposal. Your peers and I will offer suggestions as to how your proposal could be improved. You will then draft your paper, review it with your peers, and revise your draft for final submission. Before you begin and as you work, you should refer to the Components of Reflections and Keys to Reflections on pages 54-55. The chart on pages 90-91 will also help you make certain you don't forget any important steps of the process.

I will use the following criteria to assess your essay:

- Does the essay tell a good story, honestly? (Don't embellish the truth just to write a good essay!)
- How clear is your purpose in writing this reflection, and is your purpose appropriate?
- How well does it convey significance through details?
- Does the essay focus on something significant, whether great or small?
- How relevant will your personal experience be to others?
- I will also apply the Standard Grading Criteria used for all essays in this class.

Schedule
Next class: Topic Proposals due (see below)
One week later: Rough drafts due; peer review
Next class after: Peer review due; rough drafts returned
One week later: Final drafts due

Please create your Topic Proposal by doing the following:

1) Make a list of people, events, or places that have been significant in your life or in some way changed you. Conflict and resolution are often good sources of reflection. Make this list as long as you can (at least a dozen items).
2) Choose two or three items on your list and write for a few minutes on each one. Write something about how it seemed to you at the time, and then about how you regard it today. Did your initial reaction change over time? Why do you feel differently now?
3) Think about the significance of each item you've written about. Why does it remain in your memory? What details best convey its significance? Are there any conversations that you recall related to that item?

4) Look back over your writing and choose the topic that you think will make the most interesting reflective essay. You will want to choose the topic that gives you the best opportunity to engage your audience.

Write a paragraph or two describing your topic, its significance, and some of the details you will use to tell your story.

Assignment: Reflection on a Family Photograph
Based on *Writing: A Guide for College and Beyond*, page 107

Write a 3-5-page essay reflecting on a family photograph.

Using the concepts covered in Chapter 7 of the text, you will write a reflective essay about a family photograph or a specific scene you recall from your past. Your audience will be your peers in this class, who do not necessarily know much about you or your family.

Following the steps outlined on page 107 of the text, choose a photo to reflect upon that you do not mind sharing with strangers. It is not necessary to make deeply personal revelations about yourself or your family in order to write a good reflection. The photo or scene itself need not be striking; it is your memories and interpretation that will make your essay interesting to readers. Remember that if your photo or scene only elicits flattering (or only critical) memories about your family, it may not be terribly interesting to readers.

Before you begin and as you work, you should refer to the Components of Reflections and Keys to Reflections on pages 54-55. The chart on pages 90-91 will also help you make certain you don't forget any important steps of the process.

I will use the following criteria to assess your essay:

- Does the essay tell a good story, honestly? (Don't embellish the truth just to write a good essay!)
- How clear is your purpose in writing this reflection, and is your purpose appropriate?
- How well does it convey significance through details?
- Does the essay focus on something significant, whether great or small?
- How relevant will your personal experience be to others?
- I will also apply the Standard Grading Criteria used for all essays in this class.

Schedule
Next class: Prewriting activity due (see below)
One week later: Rough drafts due; peer review
Next class after: Peer review due; rough drafts returned
One week later: Final drafts due

Prewriting activity:
Divide a sheet of paper into two columns. On the left-hand side, list the different elements you notice about the photo or remembered scene: What time of day is it? Is it inside or outside? Who is there? Who is not? What are people wearing? Doing? Think too about what the photo doesn't show.

On the right-hand side of the sheet, next to each element you have observed, write a brief comment reflecting upon that element. What does it remind you of? What does it say about your family's history? Next to "Jennifer is wearing her favorite blouse," you might write, "She outgrew it the year after and handed it down to me, but I never liked it as much as she did."

Please bring your prewriting sheet to the next class meeting, where we will work in groups to review and expand them, prior to writing rough drafts.

Assignment: Reflection on the Present
Based on *Writing: A Guide for College and Beyond*, page 107

Write a 3-5-page essay reflecting on a recent experience you have had.

Using the concepts covered in Chapter 7 of the text, you will write a reflective essay about a single recent experience that you undertake specifically for this essay. Your essay will describe your experience and your response to it, and make connections for readers, showing them something unique about your "reading" of the event. Your audience will be me and your classmates, and people like us who are looking for interesting experiences and ideas to read about.

Following the steps outlined on page 107 of the text, choose an event or place to go to. While you are there, observe your surroundings and your response to them. What do you notice? How do you feel? What do you think about? What do you do? What is your relationship to this place? How are you connected to it? How are you separate from it? What about your response is unique to you? Remember that you don't have to make deeply personally revelations about yourself in order to write an interesting reflection.

Before you begin and as you work, you should refer to the Components of Reflections and Keys to Reflections on pages 54-55. The chart on pages 90-91 will also help you make certain you don't forget any important steps of the process.

I will use the following criteria to assess your essay:

- Does the essay tell a good story, honestly? (Don't embellish the truth just to write a good essay!)
- How clear is your purpose in writing this reflection, and is your purpose appropriate?
- How well does it convey significance through details?
- Does the essay focus on something significant, whether great or small?
- How relevant will your personal experience be to others?
- I will also apply the Standard Grading Criteria used for all essays in this class.

Schedule
Next class: Connecting and focusing activity due (see below)
One week later: Rough drafts due; peer review
Next class after: Peer review due; rough drafts returned
One week later: Final drafts due

Prewriting activity: Connect and focus
As soon as possible after your visit to the place you are writing about, jot down all your thoughts and observations. Record as much detail as you can about what you saw, heard, thought, and felt.

Next, arrange your notes on an idea map: draw a circle in the center of a piece of paper, and write "Myself" in it. Then, around the rest of the page, write the observations and thoughts from your notes. Draw a line from each item to your center circle, and along the line write down what connects that idea to you. Did you notice a particular face in the crowd because it reminded you of a family member? Did you stop and listen to some music because it sounded so different from anything you had heard before?

Finally, on another piece of paper, turn each "connecting line" from your idea map into a complete sentence. Read your list of sentences one after the other. Ask yourself, "Now, what do I want to tell people about this experience? How can I turn all these feelings into a story, a lesson, or an explanation?" Your answer to these questions will give you a focus for your reflection.

Chapter Eight: Observing

Be sure to access the resources available at *MyCompLab* go to (www.mycomplab.com and choose Faigley, *Writing: A Guide to College and Beyond*). Book specific features include:
* Additional "Analyzing and Connecting" questions for every reading provide a wealth of class discussion and assignment options.
* Links to bonus readings you and your students can access on the Web along with "Analyzing and Connecting" questions provide a truly wide variety of reading assignment choices.
* Downloadable worksheets that support and extend the "How to Write" process maps provide helpful reinforcement.
* Additional "Write Now," "Staying on Track," and "Working Together" activities ensure students have varied and plentiful practice activities.
* Additional Projects (major writing assignments) provide a rich source of additional assignments.

Chapter goals: We observe constantly, and this chapter helps students understand how important this single simple step is, and not to take it for granted in their writing. Much college writing (and other writing, too) would be better if students spent more time observing carefully, instead of leaping ahead to polish lackluster observations.

Chapter challenges: Students may assume that because they know how to look at things, they know how to produce observational writing. They may confuse objectivity with insipidity or flatness. Once they have developed the ability to provide a great deal of detail, they may still need help selecting detail that is relevant and vivid, instead of overwhelming readers with undifferentiated lists.

To introduce this chapter, consider having students read the sample article, "Low Wages, Strong Backs," on pages 133-141 before or at the beginning of class. They can respond to the Analyzing and Connecting questions on a sheet of scratch paper as well, to refer to during discussion.

As a class or in small groups, ask students: What did you already know or think about the subject of low-wage earners in America? Had you thought much about it? Did you think it was a problem? Do you think so now? What did you learn, if anything, from the essay? Did any of your opinions change? What elements of the essay stood out as you read it? Was it more effective than an editorial in a newspaper about the need to raise the minimum wage? Why?

Point them toward the impact of the article's detail, immediacy, concrete images, and first-person experience: these are the hallmarks of observational writing. They are generally very appealing to readers and thus useful tools for all writers.

Then read the description of observational writing on page 110. What "research" did Travers do? Note that he had a co-author. What do your students guess her role might have been? How might she have been involved in the research, writing, or revising of the piece?

Finally, ask students about situations where they might use observational writing. Have they read any observational writing for other classes, or on their own? If they are majoring in fields like anthropology, biology, or social sciences, they may have already encountered this form, especially in their readings. What do they know about the expectations of these audiences?

Writing observations

Observation is a less self-referential activity than reflection. Often though, the first person is used in observational writing, to make the writer's involvement and possible bias clear. Point out this quality of the writing for students if they do not pick up on it as they read. Many of them will have been told in the past never to use "I" in formal writing. But when the audience expects it—when, for example, a wildlife biologist must refer to the way his presence affected the behavior of birds in an observing area—the first person is not only appropriate, but necessary.

When you get to the Keys to Observations on page 111, review the Meagher and Travers piece again. How do they employ the keys in their article? Did they in fact make the writing more appealing or understanding to students reading the article? What would your students have done differently if they had written the essay?

Learning styles focus: *Working Together*

Students can do the note-taking part of the activity on page 111 in a mode other than writing. They might, for example, photograph or videotape a place (caution them that it needs to be public), or record its sounds with an audio recorder. Not everyone in the group needs to use the same media to observe their venue the same way (though they should probably choose a single medium for their summary).

Remember too that students can do this activity even if there aren't any special events or venues available—by observing the reference desk at the library, for example.

An effective observation

You can either have students read the annotated Dillard piece beginning on page 112 before class, and discuss it as a whole, or have them read it individually and discuss it in small groups, considering the keys. Dillard's essay is exceptionally vivid and immediate. Ask your students to count the number of specific incidents Dillard describes in the essay. What parts of the essay do they feel they are "seeing"?

You might also ask students to pay special attention to unexpected images or comparisons and figurative language. There is much in this essay that is poetic rather than objective; what, then, makes it an observational piece of writing?

Another possible project is to assign their paper (see the projects at chapter's end for ideas) and have them brainstorm possible topic areas in class. Group students to discuss possible topics or do this with the whole class. Then help them set up an observation and drafting schedule for their project. You might even provide a blank calendar on a worksheet that they can fill in.

Assigning and discussing the readings

There are many ways to support student learning using the readings in this chapter. You might assign one for students to read before they come to class on the day you introduce the chapter (as described in detail above). Or, if you aren't sure which reading will be most appealing to your students, allow them to choose one of the readings themselves (they are more likely to really understand the aim if they experience it in an essay they want to read).

Either way, by exposing students to the writing aim beforehand, you set your class up to discuss observational writing in concrete, rather than abstract, terms. Once they have read an exemplary observation, they will have a better sense of what observational writing really is, and the description on pages 110-111 will have more resonance for them.

The How to Read Observations questions in the box on page 117 will help students think about the context and background of a piece—why it was written, and how and by whom it was intended to be read. You should consider previewing these questions as a class.

You can make further use of the How to Read Observations questions on page 117 if you think your students need more practice identifying the purpose and nature of observational writing. Assign some or all of the questions for students to answer after they read one or two more sample essays. Don't overdo this, though. There is no need to pin down every element of every piece, and students shouldn't be led to believe that a good piece of observational writing results from simply checking things off a list.

The Analyzing and Connecting questions preceding each writing sample are another nice preview feature. Students can read these questions before they read the sample, and then think about the points they raise as they read. Students might write up informal responses to the Analyzing and Connecting questions for a reading, and then refer to their responses during a classroom discussion of the reading. Or, you can use them to spark group discussions or free-writing or journal entries about the reading. Students can answer the questions in pairs or small groups, and then discuss their answers as a class. You can also make these responses more formal, and have students submit them for a homework grade.

Use the Components and Keys on pages 110-111 to talk about the readings. (When discussing the photo essay by Ansel Adams, students may wish to consult Chapter 23, Thinking Visually, for ways to talk about visual imagery.) What background information does the author provide? How are the observations organized? What details does the author use to help readers "see" what is being observed? By looking for attributes of good observational writing, students begin to think about how they might build those attributes into their own writing.

In addition to looking for qualities that define good observational writing, students should be on the lookout for qualities that make good writing, period. As they progress through the aims chapters, they will begin to notice common qualities of good writing across genres (clarity, detail, varied sentence structure, etc.).

Additional questions for discussion of the observation samples:

- If you had written this essay or article, what one thing about it would you change?

- Do any parts of the reading not seem to fit the Keys and Components on pages 110-111? Why do you think the author did not follow those conventions for this aim?

- Which reading did you enjoy the most, and why?

- Which reading did you enjoy the least, and why?

What questions do your students come up with on their own about the writing samples?

Yet another way to use the writing samples is to have students read a pair of essays, and compare and contrast them in writing or in class discussion. They might write a brief comparison, or read the essays in advance and then generate lists of similarities and differences, as a class. Some good pairs for discussion in this chapter are:

- Jamaica Kincaid's *A Small Place* and Salaman Hameed's *The Travelogue of an Astronomer*—What point of view is each piece written from? What is each author's purpose in writing his or her observation?

- John Wesley Powell's *The First Descent of the Grand Canyon* and Ansel Adams' *Photographs of Japanese-Americans at Manzanar*—How does each piece "show" the physical detail being observed? Do the places being described seem strange or foreign to you? If so, why?

If you have time, you could also ask students to read several, or all, of the readings, and discuss the different ways they fulfill the keys and components of the genre. This will give students a sense of the many options available in observational writing, rather than focusing their attention on the limitations and restrictions of the genre.

Finally, consider using the sample readings to help students assess their own understanding of the aim. To do this, have students read one sample at the beginning of the unit, a second after they submit rough drafts, and a third when they have submitted their final drafts. Discuss the first reading in one or more of the ways described above. After the rough draft, have students read another sample, and ask them to respond to questions such as: "Does this reading give you any ideas for improving your draft?" "Does this writer use any techniques you are already using in your paper?" "If you were reviewing this reading as a peer, what advice would you give the writer?" After the final draft, ask students to read and respond to a third sample, considering such questions as "How does this writer's tone differ from the tone I used in my essay?" and "Does this author use more or less detail than I did in my essay?"

How to write an observation

The chart on pages 146-147 gives students an overview of the process they will generally follow when writing an observation. Make sure they understand, though, that charts are deceptively simple, and this one doesn't literally depict the way writers really work. Still, this chart breaks down in an easy-to-read form the many tasks students are likely to need to focus on at given stages of their project. The chart also serves as a good reminder when they are first thinking about their assignment: there are many steps to go through, and they shouldn't wait until the last minute to start.

1. Choose a subject or place to observe

Be on the lookout for students who are either over- or under-ambitious in their choice of observational site. They will need to invest quite a bit of time observing, so if they pick a location that is hard to reach, they may have problems. Likewise, a student who picks a site where little or nothing happens may have trouble finding enough to write about.

Of course, neither of these situations will necessarily derail a strong writer. But do give your class some guidance in terms of what is likely to yield successful observations for your assignment.

Audience is a very important aspect of observational writing; you will probably address it explicitly in your assignment sheet. The expectations for observational writing differ from one field to another. Don't leave students guessing about who they are writing for, or why.

Writer at Work: **Assignment sheet and topic**

Students will hopefully notice that an observational assignment can involve multiple tasks—here, the student is given at least five discrete things to observe. These kinds of questions can help them focus their efforts in the field, and their analysis of their notes later. Encourage your class to imitate student writer Megan Garza by circling all the specific elements of their assignment.

---

2. Make observations and analyze them

Check in with your students often during the period when they are making observations. Ideally, you should structure the assignment so that they must turn in some of their notes halfway through this period, so you can assess their progress, re-direct their efforts if necessary, and note which students are procrastinating.

Analyzing and finding patterns may be difficult tasks for some students, and all of them will benefit from plenty of time spent writing informally about their observations. They should not expect to immediately assemble their notes into a coherent paper. Instead, they must spend some time digesting what they have seen. Spending time writing informally about their observations is perhaps the best way to draw out what is significant in them.

You might offer or build in intervention at this point of the project, such as an in-class group discussion of current analysis, or a message forum where students post their analytical efforts and you and their classmates comment on them. This process can also take place at the rough draft stage.

Note that the two-column method allows the observer to come back to his or her notes after some time has passed, and look at them in a larger context, and in a different environment. The analysis provides a "second chance" to notice what is significant about an event. It also allows the observer to look back, over long periods of time, at observations that happened at different times. Point out to your students that this process is similar to the critical reading techniques outlined in Part One of the text. Here, they are just applied to the student writer Megan Garza's own notes.

3. Write a draft

The points covered for students on page 154 are also things you have hopefully considered carefully when designing your assignment sheet. What kind of thesis are you looking for in your students' papers? Can you write several examples for them? What point of view do you expect them to employ? Are some organizational patterns more likely to work well than others? Are some off limits entirely?

Staying on Track: Work for precise description

The points covered in the box on page 155 cover seemingly minor stylistic points, but if students follow them they will likely be surprised at how much better their observational essay is. If you comment on student observations midway through the observational period, you might point out places where they need to heed the advice here. You might, as a class exercise, have each student choose a few sentences from the draft in progress and develop it for visual detail, precision, and specific names. These kinds of changes will improve almost any piece of writing, but especially observations.

Writer at Work: Outlining

Note how student writer Megan Garza goes through several steps in order to turn her observations into an outline. Your class should not expect the outlining process to be neat. For some students, outlining may always be counter-intuitive. Stress that as long as they find an organizational strategy that works, it does not much matter how they arrive at it.

4. Revise, revise, revise

This section of the text covers the work of large-scale revision and that of small-scale editing, but as always, you want them to focus on the large-scale issues first: meeting the assignment, focusing the thesis, introducing and organizing, and concluding effectively, and providing vivid, well-chosen detail.

Writer at Work: Revising for tone

Note that student writer Megan Garza's instructor advises against the use of first person, and specifically from identifying the subjects in the observation as personal friends. Ask students why the instructor suggested this change. How does the tone of the passage change upon revision? What impression of the writer does each version give the reader?

---

5. Student essay

This finished essay gives your students a chance to look for the keys to observational writing in a non-professional piece of work. You might, as a class or individually, annotate this essay like the Dillard essay at the beginning of this chapter.

Projects

The three writing projects outlined on pages 164-165 can be adapted in many ways. For model assignments based on projects from Chapter 7, see pages 73-78 of this manual. In general, each formal writing assignment you give to your students should contain the following elements:

- A description of both the work to be done and the finished product you expect: what will they do, and what will be the result?

- A sense of who the intended audience is for the piece.

- Reference to the sections of the book and/or classroom topics related to the assignment.

- An approximate length for the final project.

- Suggested or required steps to complete the project.

- A schedule listing due dates for each part of the assignment (be sure to allow yourself sufficient time to grade or comment on portions of the assignment, and return them to students with plenty of time to work on the next phase).

- Specific criteria you will use to grade the assignment—plan to discuss these with your students as you go over the assignment (see pages 21-28 of this manual for more on grading criteria).

Additionally, you may want to include the following features:

- "Platformed" activities that divide the project into two or more segments. Platforming is usually most helpful in the beginning stages of a project.

- Suggestions for potential topic areas.

- References to similar documents that students might read as models.

Here are suggestions for assigning the projects on pages 164-165:

Description of a place (page 164)

This project will appeal to students who enjoy social activity and meeting new people. A major benefit of this assignment is that almost anyone can do it, for virtually any class. Students only have to travel to their observed location one time. Still, students will have varying degrees of mobility, so allow as much flexibility as possible in the scheduling, to give all students a chance to make their observations. Depending on your students' maturity level and the local environment, you may want to caution them to keep safety in mind when choosing and traveling to their location.

Students may need some structure to help them convert their observations and notes into a rough draft. Consider constructing a platforming activity that will move them from a list of jotted-down observations to full paragraphs. You might, for example, give them a worksheet that asks them to write down the three most interesting observations they made. Then have them free-write for a few sentences about each one. They can also look back at their notes for other observations that tie in with their chosen three. Finally, have them read through the three proto-paragraphs they have written and look for themes, topics, and connections.

This project would probably evolve naturally for most students into a personal essay of about three to five pages in length. The audience for such an essay could be people who are not from the town or neighborhood your students are observing.

To construct your grading criteria, you can refer to the Components and Keys to Observational Writing on pages 110-111.

Natural Observation (page 165)

In contrast to the previous project, this project will naturally be appealing to students who enjoy animals and the outdoors. Those who are considering careers in the sciences will find it particularly useful. However, note that students will need to be made aware of the difference between observation and research before they attempt this project. Observation on this scale is more anecdotal and less systematic than true research, and thus the conclusions that can be drawn from it are much less firm. Will your students know the science they need in order to draw inferences about their observations? If they draw incorrect inferences from their observations, will it affect their grade? Remember that observation is the skill being taught in this chapter; if students will be expected to also check their conclusions against established research, build that research and inquiry into the assignment as well.

You will probably need to be explicit with your students about the degree of extrapolation you want in their paper. What kind of language do you want them to use when they are speculating about possible causes and explanations? Beginning college students tend to over-generalize, or at least phrase potential answers as "sure things." You'll need to show them the appropriate way to write about questions and possible answers.

The list of questions described in step two of this project is a great platforming activity. Students can frequently move readily from a question-and-answer list to rough basic paragraphs, at which point they can begin to think about major organizational choices. This finished assignment could be anywhere from four to 15 pages, depending on how long students spent making observations. For first-year students, it will probably be optimal to have them conduct about three observational sessions of 30 minutes or so. On average, this will usually result in enough material for a 5-7-page paper. The audience for such a paper could be someone interested in the area observed (someone who lives or works there, for example).

To construct your grading criteria, you can refer to the Components and Keys to Observational Writing on pages 110-111.

Field Observation (page 165)

This project combines some of the appeal of each of the previous two assignments. It essentially asks students to engage in a basic social sciences activity: observing human activity and analyzing it. With six hours of total observation time, this paper can evolve into quite a long project. You will probably want to break it down into multiple steps for your class. After students have chosen their site for observation, they might brainstorm or work in pairs to think of as many questions as possible about the site. They do not need to choose a single question; rather, they should keep some of the most promising in mind as they begin their observations.

You will also want to design activities that will ensure students are keeping up with their observation schedules. Midway through the data-collection stage, for example, you might have students work in small groups, reading over one another's observations to date, asking questions, and looking for patterns that arise. They can refer back to their original question list, seeing what questions are still relevant, and what new ones have arisen.

At the rough draft stage, students are likely to need some help smoothly incorporating quotations and observations into the flow of their own words. It might be profitable to spend a portion of one class going over the mechanics of quote incorporation. If you feel they should conduct outside research to inform their own findings, build this requirement in to the assignment, and show them how such research is done.

This project might result in a very tightly written 6-page paper, or something as long as 10 or 15 pages. The final length will depend on how much detail from the original notes you want, and how much independent analysis you want from your students.

To construct your grading criteria, you can refer to the Components and Keys to Observational Writing on pages 110-111.

Chapter Nine: Informing

> Be sure to access the resources available at **MyCompLab** go to
> (www.mycomplab.com and choose Faigley, *Writing: A Guide to College and Beyond*). Book specific features include:
> * Additional "Analyzing and Connecting" questions for every reading provide a wealth of class discussion and assignment options.
> * Links to bonus readings you and your students can access on the Web along with "Analyzing and Connecting" questions provide a truly wide variety of reading assignment choices.
> * Downloadable worksheets that support and extend the "How to Write" process maps provide helpful reinforcement.
> * Additional "Write Now," "Staying on Track," and "Working Together" activities ensure students have varied and plentiful practice activities.
> * Additional Projects (major writing assignments) provide a rich source of additional assignments.

Chapter goals: Students should appreciate, after working through this chapter, the importance of audience needs and expectations in informative writing. They should have a firm sense of the steps required when reporting information—including research.

Chapter challenges: Students will often want to combine informative writing with argument or opinion of some kind, and of course, these kinds of writing often work together in real-world documents. But students must first learn to report information objectively.

If we imagine a scale measuring the presence of the author in academic writing, reflective writing would be near the top. Observational writing would fall slightly lower, and informative writing would be near the bottom. We read informative writing every day, in newspapers, textbooks, and other forms, and sometimes we even assume we are reading informative writing when in fact we are reading persuasive writing. Much of what we usually call "research" writing in college is informative. Though informative writing usually requires hypothesizing, analysis, and interpretation, it strives to remain objective and logical, avoiding direct appeals to the audience.

You could introduce this chapter by conducting an informal poll on the informative sources your class is already familiar with. They will, of course, be familiar with textbooks, but where do students get most of the information they use on a daily basis? From Web sites? Television news programs? The student newspaper? Where do they turn when they want to learn how to use an unfamiliar software application? When they can't get past a certain point in a computer game? Have them jot down the kind of information they get from each source.

Then, talk about what the various sources have in common, and how they differ. How many are illustrated? Which ones are most accurate? How do they document the sources they refer to? Do students trust some more than others to provide accurate information?

You might ask students to keep a log for a week or so, listing examples of informative writing they come across—signs, instructions, directions, etc. Unclear examples, that purport to inform but end up confusing, are especially good for discussion.

Reporting information

As you can see on pages 168-170, there are many specific instructions for informative writing. In part, this is because we are so accustomed to injecting ourselves into our writing that we need a lot of reminders to resist that impulse and focus on the task of informing. Informative writing, more than any other genre, demands that the writer anticipate any possible misunderstandings on the reader's part.

Then too, informative writing can and should be interesting, so writers must find ways to color their ideas that do not depend on drama or personality. This is a difficult task, and one that students may need considerable help with.

Students might enjoy looking through *Writing: A Guide for College and Beyond* to determine how many of the Keys to Informative Writing it utilizes!

Focus on Learning Styles : *Working Together*

After completing the activity at the bottom of page 170, students can go on to produce a short written version of their explanation, using their peers' comments to guide them. This is a good exercise for **aural learners**, as it gives them a chance to hear their ideas before writing them down. You might assign the writing task for homework, and when they turn it in ask what they thought would be easy or hard about it. What actually *was* easy or hard about it?

Effective informative writing

After they have read the Wilson piece (either in class or at home) have student refer to the Keys to Informative Writing on pages 168-170 and identify their use in the essay. In particular, ask them to notice Wilson's use of relevant examples and details. How would the essay change if these details were removed?

Assigning and discussing the readings

There are many ways to support student learning using the readings in this chapter. You might assign one for students to read before they come to class on the day you introduce the chapter. Or, if you aren't sure which reading will be most appealing to your students, allow them to choose one of the readings themselves (they are more likely to really understand the aim if they experience it in an essay they want to read).

Either way, by exposing students to the writing aim beforehand, you set your class up to discuss informative writing in concrete, rather than abstract, terms. Once they have read an exemplary informative essay, they will have a better sense of what informative writing really is, and the description on pages 168-170 will have more resonance for them.

The How to Read Informative Writing questions in the box on page 176 will help students think about the context and background of a piece—why it was written, and how and by whom it was intended to be read. You should consider previewing these questions as a class.

You can make further use of the How to Read Informative Writing questions on page 176 if you think your students need more practice identifying the purpose and nature of informative writing. Assign some or all of the questions for students to answer after they read one or two more sample essays. Don't overdo this, though. There is no need to pin down every element of every piece, and students shouldn't be led to believe that a good piece of informative writing results from simply checking things off a list.

The Analyzing and Connecting questions preceding each writing sample are another nice preview feature. Students can read these questions before they read the sample, and then think about the points they raise as they read. Students might write up informal responses to the Analyzing and Connecting questions for a reading, and then refer to their responses during a classroom discussion of the reading. Or, you can use them to spark group discussions or free-writing or journal entries about the reading. Students can answer the questions in pairs or small groups, and then discuss their answers as a class. You can also make these responses more formal, and have students submit them for a homework grade.

Use the Components and Keys on pages 168-170 to talk about the readings. What key terms does the author define? How are the observations organized? What examples, illustrations, and details does he or she provide? What does the author leave you thinking about? By looking for attributes of good informative writing, students begin to think about how they might build those attributes into their own writing.

In addition to looking for qualities that define good informative writing, students should be on the lookout for qualities that make good writing, period. As they progress through the aims chapters, they will begin to notice common qualities of good writing across genres (clarity, detail, varied sentence structure, etc.).

Additional questions for discussion of the informative samples:

- If you had written this document, what one thing about it would you change?

- Do any parts of the reading not seem to fit the Keys and Components on pages 168-170? Why do you think the author or authors did not follow those conventions for this aim?

- Which reading did you enjoy the most, and why?

- Which reading did you enjoy the least, and why?

What questions do your students come up with on their own about the writing samples?

Yet another way to use the writing samples is to have students read a pair of essays, and compare and contrast them in writing or in class discussion. They might write a brief comparison, or read the essays in advance and then generate lists of similarities and differences, as a class. Some good pairs for discussion in this chapter are:

- Hugh McManners' *Building a Shelter* and the National Parks Service's *View Lava Safely*—What purpose do the photos serve in each piece? Could the author have communicated the information without visuals? Which single image in each document strikes you as the most important, and why?

- The National Commission on Writing's *Writing: A Ticket to Work . . . Or a Ticket Out* and Lori Gottlieb's *How Do I Love Thee*—Who is the audience for each document? What is its purpose? How do the authors summarize data and research? How and where does each author make judgments or recommendations? What impact is the document likely to have in the "real world"?

If you have time, you could also ask students to read several, or all, of the readings, and discuss the different ways they fulfill the keys and components of the genre. This will give students a sense of the many options available in informative writing, rather than focusing their attention on the limitations and restrictions of the genre.

Finally, consider using the sample readings to help students assess their own understanding of the aim. To do this, have students read one sample at the beginning of the unit, a second after they submit rough drafts, and a third when they have submitted their final drafts. Discuss the first reading in one or more of the ways described above. After the rough draft, have students read another sample, and ask them to respond to questions such as: "Does this reading give you any ideas for improving your draft?" "Does this writer use any techniques you are already using in your paper?" "If you were reviewing this reading as a peer, what advice would you give the writer?" After the final draft, ask students to read and respond to a third sample, considering such questions as "How does this writer's tone differ from the tone I used in my essay?" and "Does this author use more or less detail than I did in my essay?"

How to write to inform
The chart on pages 204-205 gives students an overview of the process they will generally follow when writing an informative essay. Make sure they understand, though, that charts are deceptively simple, and this one doesn't literally depict the way writers really work. Still, this chart breaks down in an easy-to-read form the many tasks students are likely to need to focus on at given stages of their project. The chart also serves as a good reminder when they are first thinking about their assignment: there are many steps to go through, and they shouldn't wait until the last minute to start.

1. Assess the writing task and begin research
Students often are given informative writing tasks in papers and essay exams, but they aren't always clearly identified. If you often use key words like analyze, discuss, and explain, make sure students know exactly what you mean by those terms. You may think their meaning is obvious, but this is often not the case.

> ### *Write Now*: Explore possible topics
>
> If several of your students have similar interests or majors, they can do the first part of the activity on page 207 together, brainstorming out loud. Have one student act as recorder and write down the ideas that everyone in the group calls out. Then have them all participate in generating questions regarding each topic
>
> Students may benefit from writing nonstop about one topic, then going back over their list, choosing another topic, and writing about that one for five minutes as well. This gives them a bit more breadth and may help spark ideas they didn't initially associate with one topic or the other.

Help your students to be realistic in their assessment of research possibilities. They will likely have far less experience than you in this area, and your guidance can save them valuable time and effort.

> ### *Writer at Work*: Assignment and research planning
>
> Ask students to notice how the student in this example combines a search for a topic with a sketch of the logistical requirements her research will entail. Student writer Lakshmi Kotra is careful to note the amount of time she will have for each segment of the assignment, and budgets her work time accordingly.

2. Choose a topic and write a thesis

As always, remind your students that at this stage, they are writing a working thesis. They still have lots of research to do, and probably won't know exactly what their final thesis will be until they have done some drafting. They need to narrow their topic sufficiently to allow them to research effectively, but not so much that their paper is entirely predictable.

> ### *Staying on Track*: Evaluate your thesis
>
> The criteria listed in the box on page 211 can be used during peer review of rough drafts. You might also use them earlier, during a review of students' working theses. If they turn in a topic proposal for your comments, assess it for these three features in addition to any criteria specific to your class and assignment. You can also have peer groups review one another's thesis statements, using these criteria.

3. Write a draft

It's easy to get the impression that informative writing can be drafted from start to finish, without a lot of re-organization. The reverse is more often true, because informative writing has to present its information in a style and pattern that *make sense to the reader*, not just as a series of events or steps. And of course, what makes sense to the author, who has done a great deal of research into the subject, is not necessarily what will make sense to the reader he or she is trying to inform. It takes some time, and trial and error, to figure out what will work.

As a result, students will often find they need to re-draft informative writing more than they expected. You can warn them in advance that this is likely to happen, but it's also a good idea to build some time into the assignment so they can write more than one draft.

4. Revise, revise, revise

This section of the chapter address both large- and small-scale issues students will want to consider when revising, but make certain they understand the importance of addressing major issues first. This is a good point to remember yourself when you are offering feedback on drafts of papers. Do you spend more time marking surface error than you do commenting on the organization and support of ideas in the paper? Commenting in this way sets the wrong priorities for student writers. Instead, when you comment on drafts, try addressing issues in the same order they are presented here, working from high-order to lower-order considerations. Make general comments about patterns of error—comma splices, fragments, dangling modifiers, pronoun reference—rather than marking each error specifically.

Staying on Track: Reviewing your draft

Students will have a great deal to think about as they revise their informative writing. Above all, they must focus and organize their information effectively. You might want to assess, or have students self-assess, these two requirements alone before they begin thinking about the rest. The Staying on Track box on page 219 will help with such an assessment.

Writer at Work: Responding actively to feedback

Students can compare the sections of the paper presented here, with comments, to the finished paper beginning on page 222. How does the marked paragraph change from this version to the final version? What becomes of the sentences marked as out-of-place? Do students agree that student writer Lakshmi Kotra's response to her instructor's comments improved the essay?

---

5. Student essay

Lakshmi Kotra's finished essay gives your students a chance to look for the keys to informational writing in a non-professional piece of work. You might, as a class or individually, annotate this essay like the Wilson essay at the beginning of this chapter.

Projects

The three writing projects outlined on pages 164-165 can be adapted in many ways. For model assignments based on projects from Chapter 7, see pages 73-78 of this manual. In general, each formal writing assignment you give to your students should contain the following elements:

- A description of both the work to be done and the finished product you expect: what will they do, and what will be the result?

- A sense of who the intended audience is for the piece.

- Reference to the sections of the book and/or classroom topics related to the assignment.

- An approximate length for the final project.

- Suggested or required steps to complete the project.

- A schedule listing due dates for each part of the assignment (be sure to allow yourself sufficient time to grade or comment on portions of the assignment, and return them to students with plenty of time to work on the next phase).

- Specific criteria you will use to grade the assignment—plan to discuss these with your students as you go over the assignment (see pages 21-28 of this manual for more on grading criteria).

Additionally, you may want to include the following features:

- "Platformed" activities that divide the project into two or more segments. Platforming is usually most helpful in the beginning stages of a project.

- Suggestions for potential topic areas.

- References to similar documents that students might read as models.

Here are suggestions for assigning the projects on pages 164-165:

Instructions (page 230)
This is a much more difficult assignment than it originally seems to be. Students who expect to do technical writing in the future will benefit a great deal from it, but it will be useful to all your students, helping them appreciate the many possible ways to organize information.

You might begin this project by looking at examples of good and bad instructions (students can probably supply some examples of each). At the draft stage, students should work in pairs or small groups to test one another's instructions. Do they make sense to someone other than the author? What aspects are ambiguous, and how can they be clarified? After the final draft is submitted, students can test their instructions again, to see how much they improved.

The audience for this project is envisioned as a friend or fellow student, so peer groups are especially appropriate. The length will probably be the most challenging aspect for students. The idea of filling one or two pages seems quite easy, until they realize how concise and tightly-written instructions must be. This is an excellent project for working on editing and revising for clarity and conciseness. You might want to highlight these qualities in your comments and grading criteria for the project.

To construct your grading criteria, you can refer to the Components and Keys to Informative Writing on pages 168-170.

Profile (page 231)

Profiles of people are a delicate writing task. They require a certain amount of discretion and a good awareness of audience. Any student likely to work in public relations, history, journalism, or related fields will probably find this an interesting project.

Ideally, your students will find examples of both flattering and unflattering profiles as they begin this project (good sources for unflattering profiles are consumer and corporate watchdog groups and popular culture magazines). You might give students a short list of questions to answer as they review the profiles. Then, have them discuss their answers as a class. What kinds of audiences for profiles did they identify? What kind of information is provided for different audiences?

It's a good idea to schedule some in-class activity around the students' interviews, to ensure that they keep to their schedules. This can easily be turned into a platforming activity that will give them a step up to their rough draft. Begin by having them explain who they will interview, and then writing a list of questions they intend to ask. Have students work in small groups to vet their questions. Will some be too prying? Are there other questions students might ask? What do other members of the group want to know about the subject?

After interviews are conducted, you can have students write a short summary of the interview process for you. They might explain how the interview went, describe a few of the most important or interesting things they learned, and outline how they think they will structure their rough drafts.

Most students will probably spend about 20-40 minutes interviewing a subject, resulting in a final draft of about three to five pages (perhaps more).

To construct your grading criteria, you can refer to the Components and Keys to Informative Writing on pages 168-170.

Informative Essay (page 231)

This project gives students an opportunity they probably don't have often enough in college: speaking from the standpoint of expert. Remember, as you construct this assignment, that this is not a research paper, so the emphasis should not be on strictly authoritative, tested information. Blatant factual errors should be discouraged, of course, but the point of this project is to let students speak from their personal experience and knowledge; to help them develop the voice of authority, on one topic at least.

Of course, students may have trouble walking this line between expert and student. Plan to focus your comments on areas where they over-generalize or assume a tone of authority that is not justified even by their personal experience. One way you can approach this is to talk about audience response: no one likes to be lectured to, so students (and all experts) need to use their knowledge to get people interested in learning more.

Like the Instructions project in this chapter, this project will require specific attention to processes and descriptions. How can the information in the essay be organized so it is clear *and interesting* to the reader? (Quite a different challenge from writing straight instructions!) To help students over this transition, try having them start with a free-write or rough sketch of what they know about their topic. Working from this, but not reading it aloud, have students describe their topic to a group of their peers, or the entire class. Then, have the peers ask questions. What more do they want to know? What wasn't clear? This will give students some idea, before they begin their rough drafts, of how they are likely to catch their audience's interest.

This project might result in a paper anywhere from three to eight pages, depending on the amount of detail the student is inclined to provide. The audience, like that for the Instructions assignment, could reasonably be interpreted as peers, fellow students, and friends of the same age group as your students. However, other audiences might be imagined—one option is to ask students to identify their own ideal audience, based on the topic they choose.

To construct your grading criteria, you can refer to the Components and Keys to Informative Writing on pages 168-170.

Chapter Ten: Analyzing Texts

> Be sure to access the resources available at *MyCompLab* go to
> (www.mycomplab.com and choose Faigley, *Writing: A Guide to College and Beyond*). Book specific features include:
> * Additional "Analyzing and Connecting" questions for every reading provide a wealth of class discussion and assignment options.
> * Links to bonus readings you and your students can access on the Web along with "Analyzing and Connecting" questions provide a truly wide variety of reading assignment choices.
> * Downloadable worksheets that support and extend the "How to Write" process maps provide helpful reinforcement.
> * Additional "Write Now," "Staying on Track," and "Working Together" activities ensure students have varied and plentiful practice activities.
> * Additional Projects (major writing assignments) provide a rich source of additional assignments.

Chapter goals: This chapter stresses the need to think about context and purpose when students analyze texts. Students must learn how to look more closely at texts than they have before, for claims, reasons, connections, and associations. They should see that an analysis is a response to some other text or phenomenon. They should also understand the importance of asking questions in order to read texts critically—whatever type of text is being analyzed.

Chapter challenges: Some students may need to be challenged before they will analyze with the level of skill and detail required in college. Once students are engaged in analysis, logical fallacies may be problematic. They'll also have to grapple with beliefs and values; seeing their own and respecting others' may require a little practice for some students. Hopefully, students will see how skills they have already used for reflective, observational, and informative writing can be brought to bear in analysis.

A time-tested way to introduce analysis to college students is to work with magazine advertisements. These are a text students are usually intimately familiar with, and they can have surprisingly complex messages. You might begin this chapter by showing students an ad that you feel has an interesting or complicated message. Ask them their opinion of it:

- What kind of person is the ad directed at (gender, age, interests, income level, etc.)?

- What kind of product is it trying to sell?

- What "argument" does the ad make? Is it logical?

- What other tactics does the ad use to try to persuade its audience?

- What doesn't the ad tell readers?

- How is the ad designed and formatted?

- How effective is the ad, overall?

These questions will get students thinking about text and context. If the topic of consumer awareness doesn't come up, introduce it. Ask students if it's OK for an advertisement to lie about the product it is trying to sell. They will probably be aware that there are laws in place to protect consumers from false advertising. But ads do exaggerate and make claims that aren't easily supported by evidence. Is this OK? Do they ever get suspicious about a product being as good as the ad says it is? How do they evaluate products they see advertised?

Writing to analyze

Textual analysis is probably the most common writing assignment in college, whether in the composition or literature classroom. Textual analysis is also used in visual arts classes, design, history, and many other fields. Students need to appreciate the complexity of college-level analysis—that it does not mean explaining something the writer understands to readers who don't, but rather a process of taking apart, examining, and finding out. A written analysis is the final product of this complex thought process.

This chapter divides analysis into the three most common types found in college writing: rhetorical, visual, and literary. Your students will probably have already encountered literary analysis at some level in their schooling. However, they may be unprepared for the degree to which college writing requires them to support their analysis through the supply of textual evidence. In rhetorical and visual analysis too, students should be pushed to identify and refer directly to specific elements of that text in their analysis. If they make a claim, however vague, ask them "What about the text made you think or feel that?" They need to consciously list evidence rather than be satisfied with a vague impression. This will make all readers—not just college professors—take their analysis more seriously. Citing evidence is an important scholarly habit, and written analyses of all kinds are an ideal place to practice it.

Regardless of the type of analysis they will do, help your students narrow their search for a text, and intervene early as they try to formulate a thesis—perhaps by reviewing topic proposals. These two steps will go a long way toward ensuring better final papers. You may limit or guide them toward advertisements, short policy statements or editorials, poems or short stories, or visual texts that are more likely to provide fertile grounds for analysis. But remember too, that the very first key to writing an analysis is to choose a topic you care about. Students will need some leeway if they are to find a topic they can engage with.

Though we have stressed evidence and support, context is also crucial to analysis. Yet many students will need help understanding the importance of historical background, audience expectations, and the source of a text. Students are unaware of all they don't know that can inform their analysis. The best way to give them a sense of this, without overwhelming them, is usually to demonstrate. You might, for example, look at the Volkswagen Beetle design sample in this chapter and research its history and context with your students. How did a car designed at the behest of Adolph Hitler become so popular in the West after World War II? What kinds of American cars were available at that time? Where can they look for answers to these and similar questions?

Working Together

Students may have different answers to the questions in the box on page 235. This is quite natural—they are reaching different conclusions from their analysis. Help them understand that analysis is logical, but doesn't necessarily lead to a single "true" answer. Do all members of the group, for example, agree about how the creator of each text attempts to influence the audience? Why or why not?

Writing a rhetorical analysis

If you are teaching rhetorical analysis, you may have a preferred method of introducing the concept of rhetorical appeals. Aristotle's rhetorical triangle is mentioned briefly here, with its focus on ethos, pathos, and logos. This simple schema is usually fairly easy for students to grasp quickly and begin to apply in their own analyses. However, you should be sure to show students a sample of analytical writing that employs whatever rhetorical terms you are using in your class, before they begin their own papers.

Because rhetorical analyses have more varied uses than literary or visual analyses, the components and keys for this kind of analysis are slightly more involved than for the other two forms. Students will have to think more about their own purpose and audience, in addition to analyzing those of the text under consideration.

Writing a visual analysis

If your students will be writing a visual analysis, recognize that most students—even those with an extensive background in visual arts—will probably need to do some work developing their vocabulary for talking and writing about visual texts. You might plan to devote a fair amount of classroom time to discussion designed to broaden students' awareness of terms used in visual description and analysis. Many of these terms are genre-specific as well (column types discussed in architecture, painting techniques in art history), so this is an excellent opportunity to examine genre-specific writing conventions. Several sample readings from this chapter, like the Federal Express ad, Stata Center photos, and Volkswagen Beetle design guide, can be springboards for these discussions.

Visual appeals are often more open to interpretation of the author's intent or message than are written texts. This does not mean that writers of visual analyses do not need to provide evidence for their claims! But the textual evidence must be *described* instead of quoted or paraphrased.

Writing a literary analysis

If your students are writing a literary analysis, help them understand that this is more than another book report. This may be your students' first opportunity to write a literary analysis with an understanding of the critical thinking that is properly a part of the genre. Help them take their examination of text, thesis formation, and argumentation to the next level, so they have skills they can employ in future classes.

An effective analysis

After reading Tim Collins' analysis of Marie Fatayi-Williams' speech, perhaps in class, have students refer to the Keys to Rhetorical Analysis on page 237 and identify their use in the essay. You might have them consider the difference in tone between the two parts of the article: Fatayi-Williams' powerful, emotional speech, and Collins' more restrained assessment of it. Though Collins is less emotional, it is clear that he still feels strongly about the speech and about the context surrounding it. How does this obvious bias affect students' impression of Collins? How does it affect their response to Fatayi-Williams' speech?

Assigning and discussing the readings

There are many ways to support student learning using the readings in this chapter. Along with sample analysis, the readings section for this chapter also provides visuals that students can analyze themselves. You might assign one of the samples for students to read and look over before they come to class on the day you introduce the chapter. Or, if you aren't sure which reading will be most appealing to your students, allow them to choose one of the readings themselves (they are more likely to really understand the aim if they experience it in a form they want to read).

Either way, by exposing students to the writing aim beforehand, you set your class up to discuss analytical writing in concrete, rather than abstract, terms. Once they have read an exemplary analysis, they will have a better sense of what analytical writing really is, and the description on pages 236-241 will have more resonance for them.

The How to Read Analyses questions in the box on page 247 will help students think about the context and background of a piece—why it was written, and how and by whom it was intended to be read. You should consider previewing these questions as a class.

You can make further use of the How to Read Analyses questions on page 247 if you think your students need more practice identifying the purpose and nature of analytical writing. Assign some or all of the questions for students to answer after they read one or two more sample essays. Don't overdo this, though. There is no need to pin down every element of every piece, and students shouldn't be led to believe that a good piece of analytical writing results from simply checking things off a list.

The Analyzing and Connecting questions preceding each writing sample are another nice preview feature. Students can read these questions before they read the sample, and then think about the points they raise as they read. Students might write up informal responses to the Analyzing and Connecting questions for a reading, and then refer to their responses during a classroom discussion of the reading. Or, you can use them to spark group discussions or free-writing or journal entries about the reading. Students can answer the questions in pairs or small groups, and then discuss their answers as a class. You can also make these responses more formal, and have students submit them for a homework grade.

Use the Components and Keys on pages 236-241 to talk about the samples. For the analytical essays, students might consider questions such as: Does the author consider underlying values and beliefs? What connections does he or she make? What does the analysis show you that you would not have noticed on your own? By looking for attributes of good analytical writing, students begin to think about how they might build those attributes into their own writing. For the visual samples, have students apply the Components and Keys for Visual Analysis on page 238. Ask them: Who created this object, and why? What is its function? What does it remind you of? If you will be focusing on visual analysis, you can have students read Chapter 23, Thinking Visually, to help them develop their verbal description skills.

In addition to looking for qualities that define good analytical writing, students should be on the lookout for qualities that make good writing, period. As they progress through the aims chapters, they will begin to notice common qualities of good writing across genres (clarity, detail, varied sentence structure, etc.).

Additional questions for discussion of the analytical readings:

- If you had written this document, or designed this product, what one thing about it would you change?

- If you are reading an analysis, do any parts of it not seem to fit the Keys and Components on pages 236-241? Why do you think the author or authors did not follow those conventions for this aim?

- If you are analyzing a visual sample, what do you notice that goes beyond the obvious?

- Which reading did you enjoy the most, and why?

- Which reading did you enjoy the least, and why?

What questions do your students come up with on their own about the writing samples?

Yet another way to use the writing samples is to have students read a pair of essays, and compare and contrast them in writing or in class discussion. They might write a brief comparison, or read the essays in advance and then generate lists of similarities and differences, as a class. Some good pairs for discussion in this chapter are:

- Frank Gehry's Stata Center and the Volkswagen Beetle—What is the function of each object? How does its design fit its function? In what ways is the design surprising, given the object's function? What three words best describe each object?

- Alice Walker's *Everyday Use* and Dagoberto Gilb's *Love in L.A.*—How would you describe the mood of each story? How does each author communicate a sense of character? To what extent can you "see" each person in the stories?

If you have time, you could also ask students to read several, or all, of the readings, and discuss the different ways they fulfill the keys and components of the genre. This will give students a sense of the many options available in analytical writing, rather than focusing their attention on the limitations and restrictions of the genre.

Finally, consider using the sample readings to help students assess their own understanding of the aim. To do this, have students read one sample at the beginning of the unit, a second after they submit rough drafts, and a third when they have submitted their final drafts. Discuss the first reading in one or more of the ways described above. After the rough draft, have students read another sample, and ask them to respond to questions such as: "Does this reading give you any ideas for improving your draft?" "Does this writer use any techniques you are already using in your paper?" "If you were reviewing this reading as a peer, what advice would you give the writer?" After the final draft, ask students to read and respond to a third sample, considering such questions as "How does this writer's tone differ from the tone I used in my essay?" and "Does this author use more or less detail than I did in my essay?"

How to write a rhetorical analysis

The chart on pages 284-285 gives students an overview of the process they will generally follow when writing a rhetorical analysis. The steps can easily be adapted for a visual or literary analysis, by referring back to the Keys and Components of those forms at the beginning of the chapter. Make sure students understand, though, that charts are deceptively simple, and this one doesn't literally depict the way writers really work. Still, this chart breaks down in an easy-to-read form the many tasks students are likely to need to focus on at given stages of their project. The chart also serves as a good reminder when they are first thinking about their assignment: there are many steps to go through, and they shouldn't wait until the last minute to start.

1. Select a text to analyze

Ideally, your assignment will set some boundaries for students so they have a good idea of the kind of text they should be looking for. On the other hand, they will usually find more to say about a text if they have some choice in selecting it. You might, for example, ask them to choose an editorial from a newspaper in your state, written in the last 12 months. Depending on the kind of assignment and its purpose, you may wish to define some topics or texts as off limits. Students, for example, have a tough time analyzing arguments about controversial topics like gun control, abortion, and the death penalty within the confines of a short college paper. Moreover, these sorts of papers are easy to plagiarize (though the results are almost universally poor).

Writer at Work: **Choosing a text to analyze**

In this example, student writer Grace Bernhardt already had a speaker whose work she was interested in analyzing. Though these first choices don't always pan out, there's no reason for students to avoid using texts they are interested in already—indeed, such texts often result in the most engaging student analysis papers. But before they settle on their topic, students should push themselves to come up with, consider, and carefully evaluate a dozen or so possible texts to work with.

---

2. Analyze text and context

When students begin the real work of analysis, it's a good idea to keep tabs on their progress. They may need direction to keep them from going off on tangents. They may need encouragement to deepen their analysis and consider deeper issues in their text. And they may need simple factual correction on matters of context and, sometimes, logic.

3. Write a draft

Most students' first drafts of rhetorical analyses represent their initial attempt to organize the material. This first attempt, not surprisingly, doesn't always work very well. Moreover, at this stage students will often need to go back and find more evidence from their text to support their claims, consider opposing viewpoints they haven't yet addressed, or correct fallacies in their own logic. If you can get students to really think about and plan their organizational strategy before they write their draft, they will be able to focus more on these issues of content when they revise. What is more, thinking specifically about the large-scale organizational plan as or before they draft often has the added benefit of highlighting for students the essay's logical or evidentiary shortcomings.

4. Revise, revise, revise

In addition to other areas, most students will benefit from a close re-examination of their opening and closing paragraphs as they revise their analyses. As mentioned above, they will also probably want to focus on providing persuasive evidence and presenting it logically. Revision of style and tone may need to focus on their awareness of and respect for opposing views.

> ### *Writer at Work*: Revising for evidence and specific word choice
>
> Student writer Grace Bernhardt here identifies, with help from her instructor, several areas where direct quotation would make her claims more convincing. Any time students paraphrase in an analysis, they should be encouraged to try direct quotation instead.
>
> Bernhardt also re-thinks a specific word choice, "ethos," which her instructor pointed out had connotations she probably had not fully considered. Since the term in question had a specific rhetorical meaning, this adjustment was especially important for her to demonstrate her understanding of an important course concept.

5. Student essay

This finished essay gives your students a chance to look for the keys to analytical writing in a non-professional piece of work. You might, as a class or individually, annotate this essay like the Collins/Fatayi-Williams piece at the beginning of this chapter.

Projects

The three writing projects outlined on pages 302-303 can be adapted in many ways. For model assignments based on Projects from Chapter 7, see pages 73-78 of this manual. In general, each formal writing assignment you give to your students should contain the following elements:

- A description of both the work to be done and the finished product you expect: what will they do, and what will be the result?

- A sense of who the intended audience is for the piece.

- Reference to the sections of the book and/or classroom topics related to the assignment.

- An approximate length for the final project.

- Suggested or required steps to complete the project.

- A schedule listing due dates for each part of the assignment (be sure to allow yourself sufficient time to grade or comment on portions of the assignment, and return them to students with plenty of time to work on the next phase).

- Specific criteria you will use to grade the assignment—plan to discuss these with your students as you go over the assignment (see pages 21-28 of this manual for more on grading criteria).

Additionally, you may want to include the following features:

- "Platformed" activities that divide the project into two or more segments. Platforming is usually most helpful in the beginning stages of a project.

- Suggestions for potential topic areas.

- References to similar documents that students might read as models.

Here are suggestions for assigning the projects on pages 302-303:

Rhetorical Analysis (page 302)

The two main components of this assignment (both are not always obvious to students) are the analysis, and then the claim based on this analysis. Students who successfully grapple with the analytical task may be at a loss when it comes to constructing a claim based upon their findings. But both elements are critical to analysis, and students will use both skills heavily in almost any other college or professional writing they do.

It's wise to check in with students after they have chosen the text they will analyze. Limiting their choices may help them find something more likely to produce a good essay. You can give them a selection of essays, or describe a type of text you want them to work with (500-2,000 words, newspaper editorial or letter to the editor, etc.). Having them summarize their text in a half or full page is a good first step to the platforming assignment.

Prompt students to consciously analyze organization and style. These often invisible components of writing are important to their own development as writers, and they will benefit from identifying their use (successfully or not) in others' writing.

The audience for this project is most logically whoever read the original text being analyzed, but not always. Other people might be interested in, or benefit from, an analysis of a text they weren't previously familiar with. Ask your students if they can think of additional audiences for their analysis.

Most students, working with a reasonably short text, can fulfill this assignment well in three to five pages.

To construct your grading criteria, you can refer to the Components and Keys to Rhetorical Analysis on pages 236-237.

Visual Analysis (page 303)

Before beginning this project (which will appeal to students interested in design, architecture, planning, and fine arts) you and your students may wish to consult Chapter 23, Thinking Visually, for ways to talk about visual imagery. Building a good vocabulary for describing visual perceptions is a great help in producing coherent analysis.

Students may have trouble finding a claim to make about an object. Workshopping this process is a good way to make certain they get a good start on their drafts. They might start with an overall first impression, and then look for details that support that impression. The initial question, "How does this text make you feel?" can be followed up with "Why?" over and over again—the point being to send students searching for the exact elements of a design or image that made them feel that way. Encourage them to find and describe, as precisely as possible, all the concrete details that caused their response.

As they continue to look more deeply at their text, students may find that their claim changes considerably (or that it is strengthened).

It's a good idea to make it clear, in discussion and in your grading criteria and comments, that the point of this exercise is not so much to construct an iron-clad argument about the text (and especially not to evaluate it as simply "good" or "bad"—an easy error for students who get stuck on "liking" or "not liking" an image). Instead, students should be developing their observational skills, their skills at describing what they observe verbally, and their capacity to analyze, break down, and add back up qualities of a text.

Some students may struggle to get three pages out of this assignment, especially if their vocabulary for visual description is still developing. Others may produce a great deal of description but not much analysis. An ideal is probably somewhere in the 3-5-page range. Their audience may depend on the text they analyze: any member of the general public could be interested in a public building, for example. Consumers might be interested in an advertisement.

To construct your grading criteria, you can refer to the Components and Keys to Visual Analysis on pages 238-239.

Critical Literary Analysis (page 303)
This project fits the classic conception of an "English paper," and students have probably done, and will do, similar assignments. With the framework provided by this chapter, however, they will get more out of the text they read for the project, seeing it (perhaps for the first time) as a writer, not just a reader.

There are so many elements to analyze in literature, that students will probably need to do some weeding out to construct a manageable paper (five to seven pages is probably a good target length). Students will profit from some exploratory writing after they have read their text, writing about character, point of view, tone, theme, imagery, etc. After they have gotten down on paper their initial reaction to the story, they can begin to think about a possible thesis. The question "What have you discovered about this text?" will help them formulate a working thesis.

Group work for this project may vary depending on whether students are all working on the same story, or have chosen different one. Of course, you as the instructor will need to read the stories being analyzed, so it is wise not to allow too wide a choice, unless you are already familiar with all the texts they are choosing from. Students cannot be especially helpful working with peers if they have not themselves read the text being analyzed. You may need to group students according to the texts they have chosen, or find some other arrangement.

The audience for this assignment would probably be anyone who has also read the text being analyzed. You might ask students to think a little bit about who that would be.

To construct your grading criteria, you can refer to the Components and Keys to Literary Analysis on pages 240-241.

Be sure to access the resources available at **MyCompLab** go to (www.mycomplab.com and choose Faigley, *Writing: A Guide to College and Beyond*). Book specific features include:
* Additional "Analyzing and Connecting" questions for every reading provide a wealth of class discussion and assignment options.
* Links to bonus readings you and your students can access on the Web along with "Analyzing and Connecting" questions provide a truly wide variety of reading assignment choices.
* Downloadable worksheets that support and extend the "How to Write" process maps provide helpful reinforcement.
* Additional "Write Now," "Staying on Track," and "Working Together" activities ensure students have varied and plentiful practice activities.
* Additional Projects (major writing assignments) provide a rich source of additional assignments.

Chapter goals: The point of this chapter is to get students excited about tracing complex causes backwards—really, about solving mysteries. In what is probably a new step for many of them, students in college need to investigate causes with a full awareness of the stakeholders involved in causal questions. The "truth" cause of a phenomenon, even when it seems obvious, is often hotly debated. This chapter will prepare students to enter such debates.

Chapter challenges: Because they will now be called upon to investigate complex causes, the biggest challenges for most students will be over-simplification. They may analyze a problem until they have about as much material as they needed for causal analyses they have written in the past (high school lab reports, for example), and then stop. For the same reason, they may stumble into several logical fallacies, because these often seem to provide a shortcut to a "solution" in problems of causation. Post hoc fallacies and hasty generalization are probably the two most common logical flaws students will need to watch out for. Some may also have trouble identifying the stakeholders in an argument of causation; with practice, they will get better at this. As noted above, it is often a new concept for them.

Causal analysis is ubiquitous in so many fields: finance, policy, business, all the sciences, history, and more. It's an important activity for large organizations and businesses, but investigating causes is also a natural result of everyday human curiosity. Causal analysis is especially important in scientific investigation, where it must be specifically controlled through experiments, so its results can be reliably assessed.

You might introduce this chapter by giving students a causal puzzle to figure out in class. This could even focus on their immediate surroundings: Why is the room so cold today? Is the window open? Did someone turn down the thermostat? Is the air conditioner or heater malfunctioning? Or, with a little preparation you might confront them with a scientific problem: Why does a plastic straw in a glass of soda eventually float to the top of the liquid?

When students come up with a likely cause, you can ask them to think back to the cause before it. If the classroom window is open, who opened it, and why? Point out that these questions are important to ask if you want to make an informed decision about your next action. If, for example, the window was opened because a bottle of bleach had spilled in the classroom, closing the window again might not be the smartest thing to do—at least until the bleach has been cleaned up.

This discussion will give you and your class something to refer back to as you learn about John Stuart Mills' four methods of causation and begin applying them to more complicated questions.

Writing to analyze causes

Though they may seem daunting in their formality, Mills' four methods actually describe methods we use regularly to search for causes. They will help students formalize the natural, informal investigation they are accustomed to performing already. Using these methods will also head of some of the more common logical fallacies that writers of causal analyses can fall into. Run students through some additional scenarios and ask which combination of Mills' methods would likely produce the best causal analysis: Are ultra-powerful hurricanes the result of global warming? Does caffeine enhance athletic performance? Does the Atkins diet help people lose weight? Why are dinosaurs extinct?

As the text warns, most causal questions involving human behavior will not produce simple answers. Yet these are precisely the kinds of questions most students will want to explore, and they should be encouraged to do so, as these questions are the focus of much college-level research. For their careers after college, too, students need to see how to handle the complexity of causes that typifies the real world. From individuals to social systems, human behavior is too complex for ready isolation of variables (nor is manipulation of variables always ethical). Thus, methods like concomitant variation and process of elimination will be called for. You might ask your students about the hypothetical cases of food poisoning described on pages 306-307. Would it be logical to solve the problem by feeding the potato salad to someone and seeing if he gets sick? Possibly; but would it be ethical?

Causal writers must also be careful to qualify their claims. Note phrases such as "probable cause" and "it is reasonable to infer" in the Mills explanations. Definite statements of causation are rare in the real world, especially where medical and health claims are concerned. Any causes that are tentatively identified in these cases are usually re-tested independently by many other scientists, to see if the cause and effect pattern holds up.

Focus on Learning Styles: Charting Causes

The flow chart on page 309 demonstrates a useful analytical tool for all students, but especially highly visual and spatial learners. Though the chart in the example shows a completed analysis, charting can be an excellent way to explore possible causes. The writer can describe all the possible elements affecting a phenomenon, and look for ways to arrange them into a causal chain. That chain can then be tested for plausibility. Such charting can be done on paper, on a blackboard, or using a series of cards or sticky notes. The final version can be incorporated into the student's written analysis as a visual component.

You can have students try creating a chart as a classroom exercise, perhaps explaining the cause of something that happened to them personally—why they did poorly on a test, why they were late for a friend's party, etc.

In networked classrooms, you can have students research causal questions online and examine the methods various parties use to try to answer them. This is often a good way to help students discover flaws such as post hoc fallacy and anecdotal thinking. Have them search for topics like cell phones and cancer, the World Trade Center collapse, and autism. How do the various voices they find online try to explain these and other causal relationships? Which are most persuasive, and why?

Working Together

When they do the second half of the activity on page 309, students will be more definite about some of their answers than others. You can ask them to choose one question and its set of possible causes, and decide which cause(s) they find most plausible, then research the topic. They should ask: Is there a consensus on the issue? Does it match the cause(s) you identified as most plausible? If not, how different was your choice? Did your research change your opinion at all?

An effective causal analysis

After reading Stentor Danielson's article on frog deformities, perhaps in class, have students refer to the Keys to Causal Analysis on pages 307-308 and identify their use in the essay. Ask students to think about other effects that pesticides have on the environment. How do they know about these effects? Where have the heard this information? How much research have they read, as opposed to rumor, ads, editorials, etc.? Do their beliefs affect their behavior? (Are there any bottles of drinking water in the room?) Point out that we often make decisions based on causal analysis that we don't understand all that well. Causal analysis like Danielson's article lets people make better-informed decisions.

Assigning and discussing the readings

There are many ways to support student learning using the readings in this chapter. You might assign one for students to read before they come to class on the day you introduce the chapter. Or, if you aren't sure which reading will be most appealing to your students, allow them to choose one of the readings themselves (they are more likely to really understand the aim if they experience it in an essay they want to read).

Either way, by exposing students to the writing aim beforehand, you set your class up to discuss causal analysis in concrete, rather than abstract, terms. Once they have read an exemplary causal analysis, they will have a better sense of what causal writing really is, and the description on pages 306-308 will have more resonance for them.

The How to Read Causal Analyses questions in the box on page 314 will help students think about the context and background of a piece—why it was written, and how and by whom it was intended to be read. You should consider previewing these questions as a class.

You can make further use of the How to Read Causal Analyses questions on page 314 if you think your students need more practice identifying the purpose and nature of causal analysis. Assign some or all of the questions for students to answer after they read one or two more sample essays. Don't overdo this, though. There is no need to pin down every element of every piece, and students shouldn't be led to believe that a good piece of causal analysis results from simply checking things off a list.

The Analyzing and Connecting questions preceding each writing sample are another nice preview feature. Students can read these questions before they read the sample, and then think about the points they raise as they read. Students might write up informal responses to the Analyzing and Connecting questions for a reading, and then refer to their responses during a classroom discussion of the reading. Or, you can use them to spark group discussions or free-writing or journal entries about the reading. Students can answer the questions in pairs or small groups, and then discuss their answers as a class. You can also make these responses more formal, and have students submit them for a homework grade.

Use the Components and Keys on pages 306-308 to talk about the samples. What methods does the author use to analyze cause? Does the author explain the importance of the effects he or she is concerned with? What underlying causes are identified? By looking for attributes of good causal analysis, students begin to think about how they might build those attributes into their own writing.

In addition to looking for qualities that define good causal analysis, students should be on the lookout for qualities that make good writing, period. As they progress through the aims chapters, they will begin to notice common qualities of good writing across genres (clarity, detail, varied sentence structure, etc.).

Additional questions for discussion of the causal samples:

- If you had written this essay or article, what one thing about it would you change?

- Do any parts of the reading not seem to fit the Keys and Components on pages 306-308? Why do you think the author or authors did not follow those conventions for this aim?

- Which reading did you enjoy the most, and why?

- Which reading did you enjoy the least, and why?

What questions do your students come up with on their own about the writing samples?

Yet another way to use the writing samples is to have students read a pair of essays, and compare and contrast them in writing or in class discussion. They might write a brief comparison, or read the essays in advance and then generate lists of similarities and differences, as a class. Some good pairs for discussion in this chapter are:

- Ari Kelman's *New Orleans' Blessing; New Orleans' Curse* and Jay Walljasper's *If You Build It, They Will Come—On Foot*—What is the cause outlined in each essay, and what is the effect the author describes? To what extent does each author seem to think human activity is a matter of choice?

- Angela Cain's *Barbie's Body May be Perfect, but Critics Remind Us It's Plastic* and Thom Curtis' *Television Violence and Aggression*—What is the audience for each article? How does each author talk about research? How does the nature and range of sources provided by each article affect its persuasiveness?

If you have time, you could also ask students to read several, or all, of the readings, and discuss the different ways they fulfill the keys and components of the genre. This will give students a sense of the many options available in writing a causal analysis, rather than focusing their attention on the limitations and restrictions of the genre.

Finally, consider using the sample readings to help students assess their own understanding of the aim. To do this, have students read one sample at the beginning of the unit, a second after they submit rough drafts, and a third when they have submitted their final drafts. Discuss the first reading in one or more of the ways described above. After the rough draft, have students read another sample, and ask them to respond to questions such as: "Does this reading give you any ideas for improving your draft?" "Does this writer use any techniques you are already using in your paper?" "If you were reviewing this reading as a peer, what advice would you give the writer?" After the final draft, ask students to read and respond to a third sample, considering such questions as "How does this writer's tone differ from the tone I used in my essay?" and "Does this author use more or less detail than I did in my essay?"

How to write a causal analysis
The chart on pages 344-345 gives students an overview of the process they will generally follow when writing a causal analysis. Make sure students understand, though, that charts are deceptively simple, and this one doesn't literally depict the way writers really work. Still, this chart breaks down in an easy-to-read form the many tasks students are likely to need to focus on at given stages of their project. The chart also serves as a good reminder when they are first thinking about their assignment: there are many steps to go through, and they shouldn't wait until the last minute to start.

1. Make a causal claim
You might want your assignment to stress that students shouldn't expect to conclusively *prove* something their essay. Ideally, what you are looking for is their ability to find and assess possible causes, and make an intelligent, logical, and persuasive case for one cause or combination of causes. Of course, this assumes your students are making an argument from existing evidence, and not conducting independent research; however, even if they are performing a laboratory experiment, students should be cautioned against universalizing their findings.

2. Think about possible causes
Here is where you are likely going to have to push your students a bit. As in the introductory exercise we described at the beginning of this chapter, students need to continue asking "why?" even after they have identified a possible cause. The concept of a chain of causation is critical to understanding complex causes and effects. What are the root causes of a phenomenon? How do students know when they have found the root cause? Often, we tell our students to stop when they have reached a cause that it is clear something could be done about.

> ### *Writer at Work*: **Brainstorming and research**
>
> Students may need to be reminded that their final paper won't necessarily include every possible cause they identify by brainstorming. By the same logic, not every possible cause they come up with needs to be entirely plausible. These potential causes can still give them leads into useful research. Ask students which of student writer Sean Booker's possible causes seem most and least plausible to them. They can then turn to the final essay beginning on page 360 to see which causes Booker does incorporate in his analysis.
>
> Remember that causes students identify through personal experience can be useful as anecdotal evidence in a causal analysis, but they will usually need to be backed up by others' arguments and research if they are to support the writer's claim convincingly.

3. Write a draft

At the draft stage of their causal analysis, most students will need specific intervention focusing not just on the logic of their causal claims, but also on audience and stakeholders. To help get them focused on these issues from the beginning, you might require students to find at least three conflicting opinions on their topic, and address them explicitly in their writing. This may result in somewhat awkward organization, but will at least force students to investigate the broader discussion surrounding their issue.

> ### *Staying on Track*: **Look at the big picture**
>
> Students may have better luck identifying logical fallacies in others' writing than in their own. You might bring in a few examples of spurious or illogical causal claims, from newspapers, Web sites, and the like—or encourage students to look for such examples, and bring them to class to share.
>
> It is also useful to devote a portion of their peer review handout specifically to the logic of their peers' papers. Have them note any fallacies they find, and make their peer review grade in part dependent on the accuracy of their findings.

> ### *Writer at Work*: Experimenting with organizational patterns
>
> Student writer Sean Booker performs some demanding intellectual work in this example, re-imagining his paper in three different ways, evaluating them, and choosing the most suitable. Encourage your students to follow this example, summarizing the main points of the paper and the possible ways they could move among them. Which strategy will be easiest for the reader to follow, and make the best case with the evidence they have available?

4. Revise, revise, revise

Hopefully your students will not feel overwhelmed by the amount of revision their causal analysis calls for. Evidentiary and logical concerns should be prioritized; students also need a large-scale structure that will allow their claim to move forward. All other areas of revision should come after these major concerns have been addressed.

> ### *Writer at Work*: Revising for support and organization
>
> Student writer Sean Booker, though working with a fairly well-advanced draft, still notes places where he must justify his argument in the first place, provide expert evidence, and give detailed background information about the issue. These may seem like huge tasks to students who have already invested a lot of time in research and analysis, but they are necessary if all of the student's previous work is to be understood and appreciated by readers.

> ### *Staying on Track*: Reviewing your draft
>
> Students can ask the questions on page 359 not just about their draft, but about their peers' drafts. They can even apply these questions to the final version of student writer Sean Booker's essay, beginning on page 360.

5. Student essay

This finished essay gives your students a chance to look for the keys to causal analysis writing in a non-professional piece of work. You might, as a class or individually, annotate Sean Booker's finished essay like the Danielson essay at the beginning of this chapter, using the Methods and Keys of Causal Analysis from pages 306-308.

Projects

The three writing projects outlined on pages 364-365 can be adapted in many ways. For model assignments based on Projects from Chapter 7, see pages 73-78 of this manual. In general, each formal writing assignment you give to your students should contain the following elements:

- A description of both the work to be done and the finished product you expect: what will they do, and what will be the result?

- A sense of who the intended audience is for the piece.

- Reference to the sections of the book and/or classroom topics related to the assignment.

- An approximate length for the final project.

- Suggested or required steps to complete the project.

- A schedule listing due dates for each part of the assignment (be sure to allow yourself sufficient time to grade or comment on portions of the assignment, and return them to students with plenty of time to work on the next phase).

- Specific criteria you will use to grade the assignment—plan to discuss these with your students as you go over the assignment (see pages 21-28 of this manual for more on grading criteria).

Additionally, you may want to include the following features:

- "Platformed" activities that divide the project into two or more segments. Platforming is usually most helpful in the beginning stages of a project.

- Suggestions for potential topic areas.

- References to similar documents that students might read as models.

Here are suggestions for assigning the projects on pages 364-365:

Causal analysis of a trend (page 364)

This assignment will likely be particularly interesting to students inclined toward the social sciences, but almost everyone can take an interest in trends in popular culture. Key to the success of this assignment as a learning project is to prevent it from turning into mere speculation. Therefore, you might wish to add a research component to this assignment, requiring students to consult several outside sources to verify the existence and time span of their chosen trend, and to lend some weight to the potential causes. This will help to keep their arguments grounded in logic.

Prior to the rough draft stage, it's a good idea to check students' reasoning by assigning a "Devil's Advocate" activity. Have students prepare before class a list or a few pages explaining their trend and the major causes they intend to write about. Working in pairs or small groups, have students attempt to refute the possible causes. They might find flaws in the logic underlying the causal connection, or they might come up with additional counterarguments, they might find fault with any evidence the student provides (or note the lack of any evidence) for the causal connection, or, they might propose alternate causes the student has not thought of. Have the student write down these arguments, and respond to them in some way in his or her rough draft.

Depending on the amount of research you require, this paper can probably be fulfilled by most students in four to six pages. The audience could be identified as those affected by the cause in some way (a good way to get students thinking about the scope and importance of their chosen trend).

To construct your grading criteria, you can refer to the Components and Keys to causal analysis on pages 306-308.

Analyzing claims and stakeholders (page 365)

This is a rather complex assignment, giving students practice in both research and summary. It should appeal not only to students interested in public policy, but also to those considering careers in the sciences, since it will give them a sense of how even scientifically-grounded causal claims can be contested in the public sphere.

It's wise to highlight for your students the analysis of the arguments advanced for and against the causal claim they are working with, so the paper does not turn into a simple report. You might also want to stipulate a certain number of sources, so students have to do more than simply summarize some other writer's explanation of the controversy.

The initial stage of this project may take the longest, as students must research until they find a topic surrounded by sufficient controversy. They can brainstorm or subject search in pairs, or you might arrange a trip to the library for a session with a reference librarian. Checking all their topic choices before they begin drafting is an excellent way to ensure they are working with promising subjects.

Your assignment sheet for this project should spell out how much detail you want students to provide. Should they describe every source of opposition to a claim, or choose the most important or influential? How many sources are required (a minimum of three, as noted above, is probably best). Depending on these variables, students will probably need somewhere from four to six pages to complete this project. The audience might be people affected by the controversy. This might seem difficult with a case like Galileo, but thinking about the impact of causes being accepted or not accepted will help students see why such controversies are important to resolve.

To construct your grading criteria, you can refer to the Components and Keys to Causal Analysis on pages 306-308.

Causal Analysis of a human-influenced natural phenomenon (page 365)

This project will of course be of interest to any student involved in the sciences, particularly ecological studies. But many other students will find it relevant: those interested in policy, social work, health sciences, and engineering. It focuses on problem solving and requires a bit of detective work, which most students find interesting.

Depending on your students, you may want to require a topic proposal or some other method for vigorously reviewing their initial choices of topic. Otherwise, they are likely to choose something too broad to turn into a good paper—or something that is no longer particularly arguable. Focusing on a local issue may help them in this regard. Remember, though, that the project does not require them to choose a phenomenon that *might* be the cause of human activity. They need only analyze *which* human activity (or activities) actually causes the phenomenon.

The audience for this assignment could be those directly affected by the effect, and also anyone in a position to mitigate either the cause or effects (policymakers, corporations, even voters). They should think about the tone their paper needs to take to appeal to these stakeholders. Ideally, this paper will involve a significant amount of research. Five to seven or six to eight pages will usually give students enough room to summarize and argue.

To construct your grading criteria, you can refer to the Components and Keys to Causal Analysis on pages 306-308.

Chapter Twelve: Evaluating

Be sure to access the resources available at **MyCompLab** go to
(www.mycomplab.com and choose Faigley, *Writing: A Guide to College and Beyond*). Book specific features include:
* Additional "Analyzing and Connecting" questions for every reading provide a wealth of class discussion and assignment options.
* Links to bonus readings you and your students can access on the Web along with "Analyzing and Connecting" questions provide a truly wide variety of reading assignment choices.
* Downloadable worksheets that support and extend the "How to Write" process maps provide helpful reinforcement.
* Additional "Write Now," "Staying on Track," and "Working Together" activities ensure students have varied and plentiful practice activities.
* Additional Projects (major writing assignments) provide a rich source of additional assignments.

Chapter goals: Evaluation is such a natural process for most of us that student writers often want to evaluate when they should be defining or analyzing instead. This chapter lets them expand their knowledge of a familiar activity and push it to new levels of precision and complexity.

Chapter challenges: Convincing an audience to agree with their evaluation may be a new challenge for students. Moving from "I like something because . . ." to "Everyone should recognize that something is good because . . ." is a big step, requiring students to look beyond their personal opinions and find criteria that other people share. As with causal arguments, students may need to be pressed to anticipate disagreement with their evaluation.

One good way to introduce this chapter is to have students list their favorite examples of some category, such as:

- actor/actress

- band/musician/CD

- car

- book

- T.V. show

- feature film

Or, you can appeal to their inner critics by asking for least favorites, such as "What is the worst restaurant near campus?" Once you have a number of specific examples, begin asking students for their reasons: Why do they prefer one actress over another? What makes one CD better than another? Why is their favorite T.V. show their favorite? Explain to them that the reasons they are giving reveal the criteria they use to evaluate these categories. Compare the criteria of different students. Do they all focus on the same qualities? What qualities does everyone seem to look for in, say, a car? What features appeal to some people but not others?

Writing to evaluate

An evaluative claim involves more than just deciding what qualities make something good or bad. Strong evaluative writing also requires *convincing* others to agree with your evaluation. Evaluations are typically written when there is some disagreement about the quality of something—when the claim is *arguable*, not a given. Moreover, evaluative claims may focus on difference of degree: Yes, *Casablanca* is a good movie, but *how* good is it? Is it the best film of all time?

Ask students to recall some of the criteria they came up with in their introductory discussion. Which criteria were practical (the cost of a restaurant, for example, is often a consideration)? Which were aesthetic? Which were ethical? What kind of audience would find each criterion more or less convincing?

Working Together

If you don't have Internet access in your classroom, you can print out some of the examples mentioned on page 370 and bring them in—or have students do so.

You could also ask students go on to write reviews of their own—and post them if they wish. Or, have them write a brief response to a review they disagree with. Do they object to the criteria used, or to the evidence used to match the criteria to the subject? Both?

An effective evaluation

After you and your students have read Lefteris Pavlides' essay *The Aesthetics of Wind Power*, think about the following: How many separate claims or arguments does Pavlides make in this essay? What is the primary claim he is making? Why does Pavlides focus so much on aesthetic criteria? And who are the people most likely to be persuaded by his argument?

Assigning and discussing the readings

There are many ways to support student learning using the readings in this chapter. You might assign one for students to read before they come to class on the day you introduce the chapter. Or, if you aren't sure which reading will be most appealing to your students, allow them to choose one of the readings themselves (they are more likely to really understand the aim if they experience it in an essay they want to read).

Either way, by exposing students to the writing aim beforehand, you set your class up to discuss evaluative writing in concrete, rather than abstract, terms. Once they have read an exemplary evaluation, they will have a better sense of what evaluative writing really is, and the description on pages 369-370 will have more resonance for them.

The How to Read Evaluations questions in the box on page 376 will help students think about the context and background of a piece—why it was written, and how and by whom it was intended to be read. You should consider previewing these questions as a class.

You can make further use of the How to Read Evaluations questions on page 376 if you think your students need more practice identifying the purpose and nature of evaluative writing. Assign some or all of the questions for students to answer after they read one or two more sample essays. Don't overdo this, though. There is no need to pin down every element of every piece, and students shouldn't be led to believe that a good piece of evaluative writing results from simply checking things off a list.

The Analyzing and Connecting questions preceding each writing sample are another nice preview feature. Students can read these questions before they read the sample, and then think about the points they raise as they read. Students might write up informal responses to the Analyzing and Connecting questions for a reading, and then refer to their responses during a classroom discussion of the reading. Or, you can use them to spark group discussions or free-writing or journal entries about the reading. Students can answer the questions in pairs or small groups, and then discuss their answers as a class. You can also make these responses more formal, and have students submit them for a homework grade.

Use the Components and Keys on pages 369-370 to talk about the samples. What kinds of criteria—practical, aesthetic, or ethical—are used? Does the author explain or defend the criteria? What evidence does he or she provide? By looking for attributes of good evaluative writing, students begin to think about how they might build those attributes into their own writing.

In addition to looking for qualities that define good evaluative writing, students should be on the lookout for qualities that make good writing, period. As they progress through the aims chapters, they will begin to notice common qualities of good writing across genres (clarity, detail, varied sentence structure, etc.).

Additional questions for discussion of the evaluative samples:

- If you had written this essay or article, what one thing about it would you change?

- Do any parts of the reading not seem to fit the Keys and Components on pages 369-370? Why do you think the author or authors did not follow those conventions for this aim?

- Which reading did you enjoy the most, and why?

- Which reading did you enjoy the least, and why?

What questions do your students come up with on their own about the writing samples?

Yet another way to use the writing samples is to have students read a pair of essays, and compare and contrast them in writing or in class discussion. They might write a brief comparison, or read the essays in advance and then generate lists of similarities and differences, as a class. Some good pairs for discussion in this chapter are:

- David Byrne's *Learning to Love PowerPoint* and Edward Tufte's *PowerPoint Is Evil*— What kind of evidence does each author provide for his evaluation? What does each consider to be the purpose or function of PowerPoint? Are you persuaded one way or the other after reading both essays? Note the interplay between the two essays—Edward Tufte directly refers to David Byrne's. How would students enter into this debate if they were writing a third essay on PowerPoint?

- Dan Crane's *McNasty: The New "Healthy" Fast Food Items Taste Bad (and Aren't So Healthy Either)* and Stephanie Rosenbloom's *The Nitpicking Nation*—What similarities do you see in the way food and people are evaluated in these articles? Do practical, aesthetic, or ethical criteria dominate? Would you use similar criteria to evaluate food or potential roommates?

If you have time, you could also ask students to read several, or all, of the readings, and discuss the different ways they fulfill the keys and components of the genre. This will give students a sense of the many options available in evaluative writing, rather than focusing their attention on the limitations and restrictions of the genre.

Finally, consider using the sample readings to help students assess their own understanding of the aim. To do this, have students read one sample at the beginning of the unit, a second after they submit rough drafts, and a third when they have submitted their final drafts. Discuss the first reading in one or more of the ways described above. After the rough draft, have students read another sample, and ask them to respond to questions such as: "Does this reading give you any ideas for improving your draft?" "Does this writer use any techniques you are already using in your paper?" "If you were reviewing this reading as a peer, what advice would you give the writer?" After the final draft, ask students to read and respond to a third sample, considering such questions as "How does this writer's tone differ from the tone I used in my essay?" and "Does this author use more or less detail than I did in my essay?"

How to write an evaluation
The chart on pages 402-403 gives students an overview of the process they will generally follow when writing to evaluate. Make sure students understand, though, that charts are deceptively simple, and this one doesn't literally depict the way writers really work. Still, this chart breaks down in an easy-to-read form the many tasks students are likely to need to focus on at given stages of their project. The chart also serves as a good reminder when they are first thinking about their assignment: there are many steps to go through, and they shouldn't wait until the last minute to start.

1. Choose a subject
An ideal evaluative writing assignment gives students a clear sense of audience and purpose. Why does a product need to be evaluated? Who cares whether Angelina Jolie or Reese Witherspoon is a better actress? If you leave it up to students to figure out a context in which their paper makes sense, they will probably struggle.

2. Think about your criteria and your audience

As we recommended in the preceding chapter on causal analysis, you might want to require students to address one or more opposing views in their paper. This will highlight, to some extent, flaws in their logic, and will also require them to gain at least some awareness of audience and context. Looking at opposing viewpoints will also help students come up with new criteria they need to address in their argument.

3. Write a draft

Though it is very important to provide readers the context for an argument, students can sometimes get stuck on this portion of their first draft and have trouble going on to the evaluation itself. If this happens, encourage them to skip the introduction, write the evaluation, and *then* see if they can place it in context for readers.

4. Revise, revise, revise

Organization is often less of a problem in evaluative writing than in other genres—largely because the naming of criteria provides a natural sequence. However, this same natural structure means that evaluative arguments often share the same weakness: a tendency to look only at the criteria the author privileges, and not at criteria other parties might privilege. For example, you might declare your football team's quarterback to be the best in the conference because he has the best overall passing record in terms of yards. Others might point out that he has led your team to a losing season because he cannot finish off scoring drives with touchdowns. Both criteria are valid, but the student writer is likely to simply wax lyrical about the quarterback's throwing prowess, and never mention that fact that he doesn't win a lot of games. Throughout the process for this paper, but especially in the final stretch of revision, remind students of the need to address, somehow, opposing views in their own argument.

5. Student essay

This finished essay gives your students a chance to look for the keys to evaluative writing in a non-professional piece of work. You might, as a class or individually, annotate Rashuan Giddens' essay like the Pavlides essay at the beginning of this chapter.

Projects

The three writing projects outlined on pages 422-423 can be adapted in many ways. For model assignments based on projects from Chapter 7, see pages 73-78 of this manual. In general, each formal writing assignment you give to your students should contain the following elements:

- A description of both the work to be done and the finished product you expect: what will they do, and what will be the result?

- A sense of who the intended audience is for the piece.

- Reference to the sections of the book and/or classroom topics related to the assignment.

- An approximate length for the final project.

- Suggested or required steps to complete the project.

- A schedule listing due dates for each part of the assignment (be sure to allow yourself sufficient time to grade or comment on portions of the assignment, and return them to students with plenty of time to work on the next phase).

- Specific criteria you will use to grade the assignment—plan to discuss these with your students as you go over the assignment (see pages 21-28 of this manual for more on grading criteria).

Additionally, you may want to include the following features:

- "Platformed" activities that divide the project into two or more segments. Platforming is usually most helpful in the beginning stages of a project.

- Suggestions for potential topic areas.

- References to similar documents that students might read as models.

Here are suggestions for assigning the projects on pages 422-423:

Evaluate a controversial subject (page 422)

This is a wide-open topic, so decide in advance how much leeway you want to allow students in choosing their topic. "Controversial" subjects may make students think specifically of contentious issues, which are often surrounded by lots of highly-charged personal opinions. Evaluating such issues is a good exercise, of course, but students will probably need much more help cutting through the passion surrounding an issue like abortion.

To prevent students from simply quoting extensively from two different voices in the controversy, you might limit the number of direct quotations they can use in the paper. Remind them frequently that they are required in this project not just to summarize existing opinions, but to put forward their own. This evaluative claim they are making is the focus of the paper, and everything else they quote or paraphrase is there to back up their own claim. Thus, simply "taking the side" of a speaker they quote will not suffice. They must construct an independent argument.

Before students begin drafting, but after they have done most of their research, have them formalize the criteria they are using for their claim. Which are practical, which ethical, and which aesthetic? Which criteria will appeal to the audience? Which will need to be defended? You can have students workshop their claims in small groups or pairs, vetting their criteria and role-playing opposing points of view for each other.

Students can often complete this assignment in three to five pages, if they make effective, concise use of paraphrase and summary. Ask students to think about three specific types of audiences: people who already agree with their claim, people who already disagree, and people who have not yet made up their minds. Which ones are they most likely to persuade with their argument?

To construct your grading criteria, you can refer to the Components and Keys to Evaluative Writing on pages 369-370.

Evaluate a campus policy (page 423)

No campus policy pleases everyone, so this project provides an opportunity for even the least engaged students to write about something of immediate importance to them.

A natural development of this kind of argument is the development of a counter-proposal—an alternative policy that might be described in considerable detail. Since arguments for change are covered in Chapter 14, you might want to rule out counter-proposals in this assignment, if you wish students to focus exclusively on the evaluation of the policy they have chosen. On the other hand, counter-proposals are very common elements of this type of argument in the real world, so there is certainly no harm in letting students construct them here.

A good platforming activity for this assignment is to have students create a two-column list, one column containing the criteria they are using to evaluate their policy, and the other containing the various stakeholders. Students can then connect stakeholders to the criteria most likely to sway them, and note which criteria are least likely to appeal to certain stakeholders. How can those criteria be defended or presented so they are more likely to influence these stakeholders? This activity can also give students some sense of how to group criteria in their rough draft, providing a basic structure for the first version of the paper.

Students can usually conduct a basic evaluation of a local policy in three to five pages, though this will depend to some extent on the amount of detail they provide, and whether they offer a counter-proposal. The audience for this assignment can easily be described as the campus stakeholders they have thought about throughout the project.

To construct your grading criteria, you can refer to the Components and Keys to Evaluative Writing on pages 369-370.

Film review (page 423)

Fortunately, this very appealing assignment does *not* require the instructor to view every movie students write about. Film reviews are often used by people trying to decide if they want to see the movie or not, so there is no real need for the instructor to "check up" on the evaluation—this really is a fairly subjective exercise, and the real focus for students should be on providing reasons to support their judgments, whatever those judgments are.

However, it *is* important for *students* to view the film they are writing about, as they are drafting their papers. Simply writing about a film they have seen in the past will not give them the experience of looking for real supporting evidence for their judgments. You might want to construct an activity that will take place after students have had time to view their films. Have them bring in the notes they have created (if you want, you might even hand out note-taking sheets, where they must mark the time into the film when they observe certain elements). Working from their notes, have them draw up criteria they will use to begin their draft. Their observations will become the evidence that the film does or does not meet the criteria. The observations can also be supplemented with other information about the film, acquired through research.

It makes sense to define the audience for this project as potential movie-goers of approximately the same age as your students. They will probably need three to five pages to present a thorough review.

To construct your grading criteria, you can refer to the Components and Keys to Evaluative Writing on pages 369-370.

Chapter Thirteen: *Arguing for a Position*

Be sure to access the resources available at **MyCompLab** go to (www.mycomplab.com and choose Faigley, *Writing: A Guide to College and Beyond*). Book specific features include:

* Additional "Analyzing and Connecting" questions for every reading provide a wealth of class discussion and assignment options.
* Links to bonus readings you and your students can access on the Web along with "Analyzing and Connecting" questions provide a truly wide variety of reading assignment choices.
* Downloadable worksheets that support and extend the "How to Write" process maps provide helpful reinforcement.
* Additional "Write Now," "Staying on Track," and "Working Together" activities ensure students have varied and plentiful practice activities.
* Additional Projects (major writing assignments) provide a rich source of additional assignments.

Chapter goals: Hopefully, students will gain some insight from this chapter not just into how to construct a position argument, but how to research an issue so that they have a clearer understanding of it—perhaps changing their own position in the process.

Chapter challenges: Students may be apt to imitate the type of public discourse they see on television—adopting a strident stance on an issue and "arguing" it with a few talking points that do not address feasibility, cost, or opposing views. Articulating good reasons for their position, and learning to treat their audience's values with respect, are two challenges you should expect to help them meet.

An activity that may make an interesting introduction to this chapter is to have students look at some simple online "polls," such as those often posted by local news stations on their Web sites. These polls usually offer only two or three positions on an issue, and ask readers to choose one. They do not offer, in other words, much nuance into a position. Ask your students how often they see or take these polls, and how they feel about the results (if you have any experience with statistics, you might talk a bit about the margin of error for most of these polls).

Next, ask your students "What is left out of these polls? What positions are not represented? How are positions over-simplified?" Of course, the most obvious information missing from these polls is *why*: Why do people support one stance or another? Position arguments are a way for people to express the *reasons* they support a position.

Writing a position argument

A very important lesson for college students is that debates over position are not necessarily about winning or losing. Arguing well for a position gives that position a dignified voice in the debate, whether the particular argument wins converts or not. Then too, the process of finding good reasons for a position can often lead a person to reconsider his or her own opinion on an issue. Researching and writing position arguments is a way to think through important issues, not merely harangue others with the correctness of our view.

Your students likely already have plenty of positions on one issue or another, but they may not have much experience arguing for those positions in the face of reasoned opposition. If they cannot quickly convince others to see things their way, they may simply say, "Well, everyone is entitled to his own opinion!" Laws and policy, however, are formed by *consensus* in a democracy. While it is true that everyone in America is free to have his or her own opinion about setting fire to parked cars, the majority position on this act is that it is wrong, and criminal, and any person who commits it will probably end up in jail, regardless of his or her opinion.

So, while it may make some students uncomfortable to interrogate their positions on some issues (or even, in some cases, to *take* a position), it's a critical skill they will need in later life. But you should think carefully about how you will accomplish this in the classroom. It's easy for students to feel that they are being penalized because the instructor does not like their positions on some issue, or does not share their values. Be sensitive to this possibility. For this reason, you may want to restrict students' topics for writing and discussion to avoid some of the larger flashpoints that are already very culturally charged: abortion, gun control, legalizing marijuana, and similar topics tend to bring about more acrimony than real argument in the classroom. Also, because the positions people have about these issues are portrayed in the media as extremely polarized, students will have a hard time wading through the tremendous amount of superficial debate on the topic to get to real information and objective authorities.

Working Together

If you don't have Internet access in the classroom, you could easily do the activity on page 429 with other documents: political party platforms or speeches, newspaper editorials, pro and con, or dissenting court opinions are a few possibilities. Urge your students to look especially closely at underlying assumptions, and to articulate these assumptions as clearly as they can. Do groups with different opinions hold any values or beliefs in common?

An effective position argument
After you and your students read Ted Koppel's essay beginning on page 430, think about the following: What values does Koppel express? Does he seem to value privacy? Does he value safety? Where are these values implied or stated explicitly in the essay? (You might ask students to go through the essay and mark all these places before you discuss them.)

Assigning and discussing the readings
There are many ways to support student learning using the readings in this chapter. You might assign one for students to read before they come to class on the day you introduce the chapter. Or, if you aren't sure which reading will be most appealing to your students, allow them to choose one of the readings themselves (they are more likely to really understand the aim if they experience it in an essay they want to read).

Either way, by exposing students to the writing aim beforehand, you set your class up to discuss position arguments in concrete, rather than abstract, terms. Once they have read an exemplary position argument, they will have a better sense of what an argument for a position really is, and the description on pages 427-429 will have more resonance for them.

The How to Read Position Arguments questions in the box on page 435 will help students think about the context and background of a piece—why it was written, and how and by whom it was intended to be read. You should consider previewing these questions as a class.

You can make further use of the How to Read Position Arguments questions on page 435 if you think your students need more practice identifying the purpose and nature of position arguments. Assign some or all of the questions for students to answer after they read one or two more sample essays. Don't overdo this, though. There is no need to pin down every element of every piece, and students shouldn't be led to believe that a good position argument results from simply checking things off a list.

The Analyzing and Connecting questions preceding each writing sample are another nice preview feature. Students can read these questions before they read the sample, and then think about the points they raise as they read. Students might write up informal responses to the Analyzing and Connecting questions for a reading, and then refer to their responses during a classroom discussion of the reading. Or, you can use them to spark group discussions or free-writing or journal entries about the reading. Students can answer the questions in pairs or small groups, and then discuss their answers as a class. You can also make these responses more formal, and have students submit them for a homework grade.

In this particular set of sample essays, students should be on the lookout for shared beliefs each author appeals to. You might also encourage them to note the evidence and reasons each author provides. Have them think about the way an author's acknowledgement of shared beliefs colors the audience's perception of the author. More than "Do you agree with the author?" they might ask themselves, "How do I regard the writer after reading the essay? Intelligent? Reasonable? Someone who cares about the issue? Could I work with or talk to this person? What would I say in response?"

Use the Components and Keys on pages 427-429 to talk about the samples. What definitions does the author provide? What sources does he or she employ? How credible do you think the author's voice is? By looking for attributes of good position arguments, students begin to think about how they might build those attributes into their own writing.

In addition to looking for qualities that define good position arguments, students should be on the lookout for qualities that make good writing, period. As they progress through the aims chapters, they will begin to notice common qualities of good writing across genres (clarity, detail, varied sentence structure, etc.).

Additional questions for discussion of the sample arguments for a position:

- If you had written this speech or article, what one thing about it would you change?

- Do any parts of the reading not seem to fit the Keys and Components on pages 427-429? Why do you think the author or authors did not follow those conventions for this aim?

- Which reading did you enjoy the most, and why?

- Which reading did you enjoy the least, and why?

What questions do your students come up with on their own about the writing samples?

Yet another way to use the writing samples is to have students read a pair of essays, and compare and contrast them in writing or in class discussion. They might write a brief comparison, or read the essays in advance and then generate lists of similarities and differences, as a class. Some good pairs for discussion in this chapter are:

- Frederick Douglass' *What to the Slave is the Fourth of July?* and Chief Seattle's *Treaty Oration*—What is similar about the tone, audience, and occasion for each speech? What is different? What common beliefs do both authors appeal to?

- The Ad Council's *Buff Daddy* and The Center for Consumer Freedom's *Food Cops Bust Cookie Monster*— What are the advantages and disadvantages of using a visual medium to make an argument for a position? They let the author make an argument quickly, but what elements must be sacrificed to do so?

If you have time, you could also ask students to read several, or all, of the readings, and discuss the different ways they fulfill the keys and components of the genre. This will give students a sense of the many options available in position arguments, rather than focusing their attention on the limitations and restrictions of the genre.

Finally, consider using the sample readings to help students assess their own understanding of the aim. To do this, have students read one sample at the beginning of the unit, a second after they submit rough drafts, and a third when they have submitted their final drafts. Discuss the first reading in one or more of the ways described above. After the rough draft, have students read another sample, and ask them to respond to questions such as: "Does this reading give you any ideas for improving your draft?" "Does this writer use any techniques you are already using in your paper?" "If you were reviewing this reading as a peer, what advice would you give the writer?" After the final draft, ask students to read and respond to a third sample, considering such questions as "How does this writer's tone differ from the tone I used in my essay?" and "Does this author use more or less detail than I did in my essay?"

How to write a position argument
The chart on pages 460-461 gives students an overview of the process they will generally follow when writing a position argument. Make sure students understand, though, that charts are deceptively simple, and this one doesn't literally depict the way writers really work. Still, this chart breaks down in an easy-to-read form the many tasks students are likely to need to focus on at given stages of their project. The chart also serves as a good reminder when they are first thinking about their assignment: there are many steps to go through, and they shouldn't wait until the last minute to start.

1. Find an issue

It doesn't hurt to encourage students to read about several issues they are interested in before making their final choice of topic. This gives them a chance to see what has been written about it, by whom, and how complicated the issue is. The goal is not to steer them toward simpler topics, but to let them make an informed choice about the resources they'll have to work with as they investigate their issue.

Write Now: Choose an issue that you care about

The activity on page 463 allows students to begin their position argument by doing what comes naturally: saying what they think. The next stages of their project will require them to do something more difficult: explain *why* they think what they think, and try to convince others to think the same way. If you wish, you may have them consider these very questions after they have completed their free-writing: Why do I hold this position? And what do I have to say to people who *don't* hold this position? Can I envision myself in a face-to-face conversation with people who hold opposing views? What would their arguments probably be? How would I respond to them? What tone would I adopt?

Writer at Work: Research patterns

Note that as student writer Chris Nguyen investigates her issue, she also compiles a list of questions that focus on key terms she will need to define in her essay. These questions will help her focus her subsequent research efforts. Also potentially useful to your students is the smaller-larger-smaller search pattern Chris uses: she begins by researching the "smaller," local issue of a particular case at her campus. She then uses some general terms from this event—T-shirts, free speech, arrest— to search for more general sources addressing the legal considerations in the case.

By reading these "larger," wider-ranging sources, Chris found references to cases similar to the one at her school. She then researched some of these to find out how they compared with her local case, and what the outcome was for each. This strategy gave her a wealth of detailed examples to refer to in her argument.

---

2. Develop reasons and write a working thesis

Developing and supporting reasons for their argument will be far and away the biggest challenge for most students. Note too that if a student does come up with many reasons for his or her position, he or she is then likely to have trouble organizing the argument! This is a good stage in which to have students work slowly and carefully with each other, and with you, to vet each of their reasons, and to search for additional ones. Students can often help one another a great deal in the task of anticipating objections and thinking of types of supporting evidence that are needed.

Staying on Track: Evaluate your thesis

Your students may not have a well-developed sense of what is manageable, arguable, and sufficiently specific in terms of a working thesis, so give them feedback on this point early. It will save you and them a lot of time and trouble later. You might evaluate their theses yourself, or have students work in groups, asking one another the questions on page 467.

Writer at Work: Finding and organizing evidence

Perhaps because her topic concerns constitutional rights, student writer Chris Nguyen eventually hits on the idea of arguing her case from precedent—finding cases where judges and juries had agreed with her interpretation of the law, and then showing how her case was similar to those cases. This is also a form of definitional argument: if Chris can establish that her case meets the criteria established by the courts for protected free speech, then it is clear that the school administrators overstepped their bounds.

---

3. Write a draft

As mentioned above, students may need more than one drafting session in order to determine the best structure for their position argument. In addition to laying out their own reasons, supplying evidence to support them, and avoiding fallacies—none of them simple tasks—students must also incorporate relevant counter-arguments to their position. Because of the complex nature of position arguments, you may wish to divide the drafting process into two discrete stages: one focused on evidence, support, and logic, and the other on audience and opposition.

Staying on Track: Facts vs. your opinion

The kind of research recommended on page 471 is an excellent exercise for almost any "belief" you or your students hold. Rather than disputing problematic claims in student drafts, you might instead require the writer to do some additional research into the claim. If students seem determined to only acknowledge sources that support their claims, and ignore other evidence, try randomly pairing students and having them research each other's claims.

> ### *Writer at Work*: Idea mapping
>
> Student writer Chris Nguyen began thinking about the organization of the body of her paper by listing the particular case she was interested in, as well as the similar cases she had found during her research. She then carefully articulated the factors those cases had in common. She then had several options. One was to discuss each case in turn, including the relevant court decisions. Another was to discuss her school's case in detail, bringing in the other cases to illustrate what aspects of it had already been deemed unconstitutional by the courts.
>
> The option she chose combined some aspects of the preceding structural patterns: she opened with brief discussions of the local case and the other cases, summarizing the factors all the cases had in common. Then, she addressed the four factors she had set up, comparing her local case with the other case, factor by factor. This strategy worked well for Chris' paper because no single case she had found exactly mirrored what had happened at her school. Using the common factors as an organizational pattern allowed her to move back and forth between the cases without losing her readers' focus.

4. Revise, revise, revise

Try not to let your students get discouraged if they have a lot of major organizational or evidentiary work to do when they revise. Any position that is worth arguing for is probably complex. What they are working for at this stage is to give their ideas and research the presentation they deserve.

> ### *Writer at Work*: Placing your claim
>
> The rather simple suggestion that Chris move her topic sentence to the end of the opening paragraph is illustrative of the kind of re-thinking writers often have trouble doing on their own. After working long and hard on a draft, it becomes hard to see it any differently. This is where a second set of eyes is invaluable. Writing center tutors are specifically trained to help students "re-see" their writing, but working with peers can help them find these kinds of solutions too.

5. Student essay

This finished essay gives your students a chance to look for the keys to position arguments in a non-professional piece of work. You might, as a class or individually, annotate this essay like the Koppel essay at the beginning of this chapter.

Projects

The three writing projects outlined on pages 482-483 can be adapted in many ways. For model assignments based on projects from Chapter 7, see pages 73-78 of this manual. In general, each formal writing assignment you give to your students should contain the following elements:

- A description of both the work to be done and the finished product you expect: what will they do, and what will be the result?

- A sense of who the intended audience is for the piece.

- Reference to the sections of the book and/or classroom topics related to the assignment.

- An approximate length for the final project.

- Suggested or required steps to complete the project.

- A schedule listing due dates for each part of the assignment (be sure to allow yourself sufficient time to grade or comment on portions of the assignment, and return them to students with plenty of time to work on the next phase).

- Specific criteria you will use to grade the assignment—plan to discuss these with your students as you go over the assignment (see pages 21-28 of this manual for more on grading criteria).

Additionally, you may want to include the following features:

- "Platformed" activities that divide the project into two or more segments. Platforming is usually most helpful in the beginning stages of a project.

- Suggestions for potential topic areas.

- References to similar documents that students might read as models.

Here are suggestions for assigning the projects on pages 482-483:

Position argument (page 482)

This project presents the same potential pitfall as the first Causal project in the previous chapter: "Controversial" issues may make students think specifically of contentious issues, which are often surrounded by lots of highly-charged personal opinions. With this project, plan to spend some time helping students navigate between the emotions attached to an issue and the claims and reasons that support the various positions.

You will probably want to review students' topics early in the project, to make sure they are both manageable and arguable. Analyzing stakeholders is a good way to find out if a claim is really controversial. If one position would benefit everyone, no one is going to disagree with it. A good activity to check for arguability is to have students list everyone affected by their issue, in as much detail as possible, and then assess what each person or group stands to lose or gain from their position. This can be done as part of a topic proposal, and turned into the opening section of their rough draft, where they will likely summarize their issue.

In terms of length, more is not always better in an argument of this type. Assigning a length of about three to five pages will force students to be concise in presenting their own opinions, and in summarizing others' positions.

To construct your grading criteria, you can refer to the Components and Keys to Position Arguments on pages 427-429.

Rebuttal argument (page 483)

This assignment might make a nice alternative to the previous one, if students have trouble constructing an entire position of their own. Reacting to someone else's argument provides them with a basic structure for their own argument to follow. Rebuttal is also a common and necessary form of public and professional writing, so the project will be useful to them in the future, too.

This assignment will help students break down the elements of a position argument: What is the claim? What are the facts supplied? What are the assumptions? Students might begin their rebuttal by identifying and listing each of these elements on a worksheet, and then responding to each, using the questions on page 483. Point out to students that they don't have to disagree with every aspect of the argument they are rebutting. In fact, pointing to areas of agreement with the author being rebutted is an excellent strategy for winning an audience's trust.

Depending on the length of the argument being refuted, you can expect this project to develop into a 4-6-page paper. This assumes a fair amount of detail in the student's analysis of the original argument. The audience is most likely the same audience to whom the original argument was addressed.

To construct your grading criteria, you can refer to the Components and Keys to Position Arguments on pages 427-429.

Narrative position argument (page 483)

This project may remind students of the reflective writing they have done for Chapter 7, and indeed it will contain many elements of reflective writing. What is added here is the analysis of cause and the establishment of a position supported by evidence and reasons.

The jump from personal experience to position argument requires students to understand the power and the limits of anecdotal evidence. To help them make this transition, you might focus, in their rough drafts, on the argument that will probably come after their description of the event. For peer review, consider having students focus on this element of their papers, using a worksheet or set of questions. You want them to consider:

- To what extent can their personal experience be generalized to others?

- What evidence can they draw upon to show that their problem likely affects other people?

- How might someone with a different experience respond to your claim?

The audience for this project should purposely be defined as larger than just those who have had similar experiences. Who are the people who have given rise to the conditions described in the essay? Who are the people able to change the situation?

Students can probably fulfill this assignment in three to five pages, but since they are writing about personal experience, don't be surprised if they expand to four to six pages. Writing about personal experience usually boosts writers' fluency significantly.

To construct your grading criteria, you can refer to the Components and Keys to Position Arguments on pages 427-429.

Be sure to access the resources available at *MyCompLab* go to
(www.mycomplab.com and choose Faigley, *Writing: A Guide to College and Beyond*). Book specific features include:
* Additional "Analyzing and Connecting" questions for every reading provide a wealth of class discussion and assignment options.
* Links to bonus readings you and your students can access on the Web along with "Analyzing and Connecting" questions provide a truly wide variety of reading assignment choices.
* Downloadable worksheets that support and extend the "How to Write" process maps provide helpful reinforcement.
* Additional "Write Now," "Staying on Track," and "Working Together" activities ensure students have varied and plentiful practice activities.
* Additional Projects (major writing assignments) provide a rich source of additional assignments.

Chapter goals: Students should come away from this chapter with a working knowledge of the nuts-and-bolts components of arguments for change, and—perhaps even more importantly—a sense of the importance of proposal arguments in the world beyond college.

Chapter challenges: In addition to all the work required when arguing for a position, an argument for change requires motivational skill. The writer is trying to get his or her audience to act, not just think differently. This is difficult even for excellent writers; it may be a daunting task for some of your students. And yet, as the text points out, virtually every major endeavor we are familiar with began when somebody proposed doing it—and convinced others it was worth doing.

This chapter truly launches students into real-world writing. So many important documents in the work world are written in proposal form that it is almost impossible to enumerate them all. The breadth of sample proposal arguments in this chapter should give students some idea, though: have them look through these examples briefly as you introduce the chapter. You could ask them to think about which of these kinds of documents they can picture themselves writing five or 10 years from now. Do they expect their professional life to involve writing grant proposals? Promotional material? Government policy? What kinds of proposals are typically made in the fields they are interested in?

Making an argument for change
Specificity is an important element of proposal arguments, and one you would do well to point out to your students early. Ringing calls for change are all well and good, but if the audience doesn't understand exactly what is being proposed, how it will solve the problem, and how much it will cost, it will be hard to win them over.

After students complete the exercise on page 489, you could have the groups go on to propose brief solutions to each problem on their lists. Then have them rank the possible solutions by difficulty, cost, or complexity. Which solutions would be most difficult to enact? Finally, ask them to compare their rankings of solutions with their previous ranking of problems' importance.

An effective argument for change

After reading the Declaration of Independence, beginning on page 490, ask your students if they know how it was distributed. Who was the intended audience for this document? While we Americans naturally think of the Declaration as an eminently convincing proposal argument, the fact is that it did not, by itself, persuade England's King George III or his government to concede the American colonies their independence. To achieve that, military action was required. Is the Declaration, then, a failed proposal argument? Or did its signers have in mind another audience beyond King George and his Parliament?

Assigning and discussing the readings

There are many ways to support student learning using the readings in this chapter. You might assign one for students to read before they come to class on the day you introduce the chapter. Or, if you aren't sure which reading will be most appealing to your students, allow them to choose one of the readings themselves (they are more likely to really understand the aim if they experience it in an essay they want to read).

Either way, by exposing students to the writing aim beforehand, you set your class up to discuss arguments for change in concrete, rather than abstract, terms. Once they have read an exemplary proposal argument, they will have a better sense of what an argument for change really is, and the description on pages 486-489 will have more resonance for them.

The How to Read Arguments for Change questions in the box on page 495 will help students think about the context and background of a piece—why it was written, and how and by whom it was intended to be read. You should consider previewing these questions as a class.

You can make further use of the How to Read Arguments for Change questions on page 495 if you think your students need more practice identifying the purpose and nature of proposal arguments. Assign some or all of the questions for students to answer after they read one or two more sample essays. Don't overdo this, though. There is no need to pin down every element of every piece, and students shouldn't be led to believe that a good proposal argument results from simply checking things off a list.

The Analyzing and Connecting questions preceding each writing sample are another nice preview feature. Students can read these questions before they read the sample, and then think about the points they raise as they read. Students might write up informal responses to the Analyzing and Connecting questions for a reading, and then refer to their responses during a classroom discussion of the reading. Or, you can use them to spark group discussions or free-writing or journal entries about the reading. Students can answer the questions in pairs or small groups, and then discuss their answers as a class. You can also make these responses more formal, and have students submit them for a homework grade.

Use the Components and Keys on pages 486-489 to talk about the samples. Are the problem and proposed solution clear? Does the solution seem feasible, and better than other options? Are any possible side effects explored? By looking for attributes of good proposal arguments, students begin to think about how they might build those attributes into their own writing.

In addition to looking for qualities that define good proposal arguments, students should be on the lookout for qualities that make good writing, period. As they progress through the aims chapters, they will begin to notice common qualities of good writing across genres (clarity, detail, varied sentence structure, etc.).

Additional questions for discussion of the sample proposal arguments:

- If you had written this document, what one thing about it would you change?

- Do any parts of the reading not seem to fit the Keys and Components on pages 486-489? Why do you think the author or authors did not follow those conventions for this aim?

- Which of the readings would be most likely to make *you* act? Which is least likely to move you to action? Is this due more to qualities in the essays themselves, or to your existing personal beliefs and opinions?

- Which reading did you enjoy the most, and why?

- Which reading did you enjoy the least, and why?

What questions do your students come up with on their own about the writing samples?

Yet another way to use the writing samples is to have students read a pair of essays, and compare and contrast them in writing or in class discussion. They might write a brief comparison, or read the essays in advance and then generate lists of similarities and differences, as a class. Some good pairs for discussion in this chapter are:

- Richard Nixon's speech *Building the Interstate Highway System* and the Monteray County Fire Chiefs Association's grant proposal *Breaking the Fire Department's Language Barrier*—Why do these two proposal provide so much detail? Who is the audience for each piece, and what is its ultimate purpose?

- The U.S Armed Forces' Marine Corps Recruitment Web site and Nancy Clark's *Mirror, Mirror on the Wall . . . Are Muscular Men the Best of All?*—How do ideal images of masculinity shape each of these arguments? What problem does each piece attempt to solve?

If you have time, you could also ask students to read several, or all, of the readings, and discuss the different ways they fulfill the keys and components of the genre. This will give students a sense of the many options available in proposal arguments, rather than focusing their attention on the limitations and restrictions of the genre.

Finally, consider using the sample readings to help students assess their own understanding of the aim. To do this, have students read one sample at the beginning of the unit, a second after they submit rough drafts, and a third when they have submitted their final drafts. Discuss the first reading in one or more of the ways described above. After the rough draft, have students read another sample, and ask them to respond to questions such as: "Does this reading give you any ideas for improving your draft?" "Does this writer use any techniques you are already using in your paper?" "If you were reviewing this reading as a peer, what advice would you give the writer?" After the final draft, ask students to read and respond to a third sample, considering such questions as "How does this writer's tone differ from the tone I used in my essay?" and "Does this author use more or less detail than I did in my essay?"

How to write an argument for change

The chart on pages 522-523 gives students an overview of the process they will generally follow when writing an argument for change. Make sure students understand, though, that charts are deceptively simple, and this one doesn't literally depict the way writers really work. Still, this chart breaks down in an easy-to-read form the many tasks students are likely to need to focus on at given stages of their project. The chart also serves as a good reminder when they are first thinking about their assignment: there are many steps to go through, and they shouldn't wait until the last minute to start.

If you have not already introduced your students to Part Three of *Writing: A Guide for College and Beyond*, they will certainly need its information on research as they write their argument for change. Research—for feasibility especially—is an important component in almost all proposal arguments.

1. Identify the problem

As with all other claims students generate at the beginning of writing projects, they should regard their initial proposal as a working thesis—a tool to guide their research and thinking as they investigate the problem further. Later on, they may decide to change their proposal slightly, or a lot—or even to abandon it entirely in favor of another approach. If their research does not support the proposal they start out with, there is little point in going through the motions of trying to persuade others to accept it. Instead, they should think about what they have learned during research that changed their minds about the thesis, and adapt their thesis accordingly. Informing and persuading audiences is not the only benefit of writing. As they research and write, authors often find themselves becoming more informed as well.

Focus on Learning Styles: Make an Idea Map

The idea map pictured on page 525 is an ideal method for visual-spatial learners, but can also be productive for students with other preferred learning styles. The following headings and solutions can be used for just about any proposal claim: Problem, Solution, How would it work? Who would support? Who would oppose? How long would it take? Pro arguments, and Counter-arguments. "Cost" and "Who will pay?" might not be bad categories to add in many cases as well.

***Writer at Work*: Evaluating your ideas**

Student writer Kim Lee not only sketches out several possible topics for her proposal argument, she also notes some of the plusses and minuses associated with each. This metacommentary helps her sort through her potential topics and focus on the one that she believes will be easiest to motivate audiences on.

2. Propose your solution

As we noted above, specificity is crucial in proposal arguments, and it's best if students aim to be specific from the very beginning. If you have them turn in topic proposals for comments before they write their drafts, use the questions on specificity and feasibility especially to show them where they still need to flesh out their proposal.

***Staying on Track*: Acknowledging other points of view**

The give and take of civil debate is modeled all too infrequently in the public sphere, so students may need extra help in striking the right tone for a proposal. This is one area where you might consider giving explicit instructions as to audience on their assignment sheets. Students might, for example, be required to write to an audience that they know does not agree with them. If they don't want to completely waste their efforts, then, they will have to treat opposing positions fairly, and argue persuasively.

3. Write a draft

Compared to arguments for a position (see Chapter 13), arguments for change can usually be structured fairly simply. The information they contain may be quite complex, so a straightforward presentation style helps readers keep track of all the details. Students might address alternate proposals or opposition in either the section where they detail the proposed solution (explaining how theirs differs from, and excels, other proposed solutions), or in the feasibility section (where they might argue that, contrary to some opinions, their proposal is feasible—or that it is more feasible than other proposals).

```
┌─────────────────────────────────────────────────────────┐
│         Writer at Work: Outlining a proposal draft      │
│                                                         │
│ Student writer Kim Lee was able to produce a detailed   │
│ working outline for her argument. Other students may    │
│ find it difficult to work in this way, and prefer idea  │
│ mapping or simply writing a "zero draft" and then       │
│ drastically re-organizing their ideas once they see     │
│ what they have said. Any way a student can find to get  │
│ an overall picture of his or her argument—a picture     │
│ that can be mentally re-arranged to find the best       │
│ structure—is a good process.                            │
└─────────────────────────────────────────────────────────┘
```

4. Revise, revise, revise

By this stage most students should have an acceptable framework for their proposal and can focus on the logic, reasons, and support they provide throughout. Since they are trying to persuade a neutral or even hostile audience, there will almost always be more they can do to bolster their claims, clarify processes, or demonstrate the importance of the problem they are addressing.

> ### *Writer at Work*: Revising for focus
>
> The weak points that student writer Kim Lee identifies in her draft are typical of those found in many student papers: after spending a great deal of time and energy researching and thinking about the topic, students' rough drafts may contain vestigial ideas that helped get them to the draft stage but aren't needed in the final proposal. Some of these ideas can simply be eliminated; others can still provide useful background or color to the argument if they are worked into the argument with appropriate placement and transitions.

> ### *Staying on Track*: Reviewing your draft
>
> Encourage students—whether they are reviewing their own papers or their peers'—to be skeptical reviewers. To do the most good, they should try to think like a voter, taxpayer, or other stakeholder in whatever the problem and proposed solution are.

5. Student essay

This finished essay gives your students a chance to look for the keys to proposals for change in a non-professional piece of work. You might, as a class or individually, annotate this essay like the Declaration of Independence at the beginning of this chapter.

Projects

The three writing projects outlined on pages 544-545 can be adapted in many ways. For model assignments based on projects from Chapter 7, see pages 73-78 of this manual. In general, each formal writing assignment you give to your students should contain the following elements:

- A description of both the work to be done and the finished product you expect: what will they do, and what will be the result?

- A sense of who the intended audience is for the piece.

- Reference to the sections of the book and/or classroom topics related to the assignment.

- An approximate length for the final project.

- Suggested or required steps to complete the project.

- A schedule listing due dates for each part of the assignment (be sure to allow yourself sufficient time to grade or comment on portions of the assignment, and return them to students with plenty of time to work on the next phase).

- Specific criteria you will use to grade the assignment—plan to discuss these with your students as you go over the assignment (see pages 21-28 of this manual for more on grading criteria).

Additionally, you may want to include the following features:

- "Platformed" activities that divide the project into two or more segments. Platforming is usually most helpful in the beginning stages of a project.

- Suggestions for potential topic areas.

- References to similar documents that students might read as models.

Here are suggestions for assigning the projects on pages 544-545:

Proposal essay (page 544)

Building on the evaluative projects in Chapter 12, this assignment asks students to focus specifically on a proposal to solve an identified problem. Proposals make up a huge proportion of professional writing, so almost any student will benefit from attempting this project.

Research is key in this project. Students will need persuasive evidence that their problem affects enough people to be important. They will need to correctly identify who can enact their proposal. They will need to document the expected cost. And they must deal with any likely counter-proposals. We suggest breaking out these four areas in a separate research assignment, after they have chosen their topics. The evidence they gather in response can then be assessed by you and/or peers, and weak areas addressed before drafting begins.

Be aware that students are apt to over-estimate the number of other people affected by problems that affect them. They are also likely to under-estimate the probably cost of enacting their proposal. Encourage them to check these areas of their paper carefully. You should also build into your assignment grading criteria directly addressing the specificity and detail of their proposed solution. This will prevent another common response to difficult problems: the proposal to "bring in experts to study and solve the problem."

To adequately address all elements of this project, most students will need at least five to seven pages. The audience would probably consist of several groups: Those affected by the problem, those responsible for implementing it, and, in the case of public works, those who will be paying for it.

To construct your grading criteria, you can refer to the Components and Keys to Proposal Arguments on pages 486-489.

Reconstructing a proposal (page 545)

Students may have the best luck finding a topic for this project if they look for something that doesn't seem to be functioning well—a mall that no one shops at, a traffic intersection that's always gridlocked, etc. Or, they may become curious about why something is designed a certain way, because it isn't obvious: Why exactly do most states observe Daylight Savings Time? Why do we have an electoral college?

One realization students should come to through this project is the extent to which an initial proposal can be altered by the compromises that various stakeholders demand. This is one reason some solutions lose effectiveness as they are implemented. To help them understand this important point, early in the project, have your students bring in a few pages of writing about the problem they think lay behind their policy, building, etc. Ask them to describe the problem aloud to the class as a whole, and then discuss: What other issues do they think may have affected the proposal and its implementation? Who were the stakeholders? What compromises might have been struck, and why? Note that for the purposes of this assignment, the historical record of the initial policy and stakeholders is not crucial. Students may research these issues, but they will get just as much out of trying to recreate the situation on their own.

A good target length for this assignment is probably about four to five pages, allowing four to five pages for the recreated proposal. The audience can be envisioned as anyone affected by the proposal's implementation, whether effective or not, and also anyone confronting a similar problem, who might learn from past successes and mistakes.

To construct your grading criteria, you can refer to the Components and Keys to Proposal Arguments on pages 486-489.

Teamwork: Counter-proposal (page 545)

Another realistic project, this assignment closely resembles writing that many professionals do on a daily basis. To turn it into a single submission, have your teams package their counter-proposals together with a summary, written by the group, of the original proposal, as well as an overview of the various counter-proposals they have come up with. The summary should use the components of proposals outlined in the chapter: describing the problem, outlining the solution, and arguing for its fairness and feasibility.

You might also consider having the groups present their summary and counter-proposals orally. The entire class could then vote on which counter-proposal is most appealing (or if none is more appealing than the original). The class, in voting, should take into account the likely audience for such counter-proposals—probably whoever is affected by the original proposal.

Total length for this assignment will probably be approximately one to two pages for the summary, one page for the overview, and one to two pages for each counter-proposal.

To construct your grading criteria, you can refer to the Components and Keys to Proposal Arguments on pages 486-489.

PART THREE: THE WRITER AS RESEARCHER

Part Three of *Writing: A Guide for College and Beyond* gives students detailed information on every aspect of research to support their writing. They will most likely need the information here in conjunction with a project from one of the aims chapters in Part Two. You might want to schedule these chapters into your syllabus at the point where students will begin thinking about outside research for their papers.

Throughout the chapters in this section, a Researcher at Work feature tracks the progress of student writer George Abukar as he develops a research topic, investigates his issues, and drafts and revises the final paper. Chapter 21 depicts the culmination of the student research process, with George's completed paper provided in full.

Chapter Fifteen: Planning Research

> Be sure to access the resources available at *MyCompLab* go to (www.mycomplab.com and choose Faigley, *Writing: A Guide to College and Beyond*) to find helpful resources including Research Navigator as well as extensive instruction and activities for evaluating sources and avoiding plagiarism.

Chapter goals: Though no one begins a research project knowing what he or she will find out, it still helps to have some sort of plan by which to structure your efforts. This chapter should help students understand some of the ways they can manage their research process, to get the most out of it.

Chapter challenges: Over-planning their research may lead some students to short-change their initial attempts at broad inquiry. Just as editing too soon can cause students to skip over needed large-scale revisions, they may have a tendency to map out research that is simple, logistically easy to manage—and largely useless.

Analyze the research task

Since college students are still learning what kinds of research are expected or required for different writing projects, it will help a lot if you think about the "goals" on page 549 when you create your assignment sheets. Often, professors expect students to know what they mean by words like "discuss," "investigate," "survey," and so on. But the truth is these words can mean different things from person to person, discipline to discipline. Delineate the type and extent of research you expect in the assignment, and what you expect your students to do with it. Talk with your class about questions like these:

- What constitutes an acceptable source for this assignment? What sources will not be acceptable?

- To what extent should your students extrapolate from the data, or interpret their findings?

- Do you expect them to generate conjectural or speculative claims, perhaps at the end of their paper?

- What kind of language should they use to make such claims?

- Will some parts of the assignment require more research and support than others? Which ones?

Ask a question

As students look for a subject to write about, give them time and opportunity to explore, but also make sure they really are doing—not just procrastinating. You might create some short take-home assignments or in-class work to keep them focused on this task.

On the other hand, some students are uncomfortable with the uncertainty of not having a topic, and will seize on the first likely one they come across—often with poor final results. Do a class activity like online subject searching or in-class brainstorming to prod them into inquiry. Students need to learn to enjoy, not fear, this process. (In fact, you might remind them that the Internet was developed to help researchers share data.)

In the end, what you hope students will see is that research does not mean simply looking up a few facts which happen to fit with a conclusion you have already decided upon. The assumption that they should be finding rote answers to routine questions is what makes the research process seem pointless to many students. So take the time to help them devise good research questions, which will require active research and questioning. They will learn much more from the work they—and you—put into the assignment.

Determine what you need

Once students have a topic and a workable line of inquiry, they can start to get a sense of what they'll probably need to do. A good way to platform the transition from issue to research plan is to have students first answer the questions on page 551, and then sketch out a research calendar for their topic like the ones shown on page 552. You can do this as two separate assignments, perhaps even collecting the first set of answers and providing feedback before they go on to build a schedule.

Draft a working thesis

Experienced writers tinker with their thesis as they research, as a matter of course. This process may not be as obvious to student writers, who are sometimes inclined to disregard any research findings that don't support the very first thesis they construct. Or, sometimes they are driven to despair when they find information that doesn't support their thesis, and want to change topics entirely. Instead, explain to them that a working thesis can and should evolve as the research goes forward, in response to what they find as they research.

Write Now: **Determine what information you need**

After they draft their lists for the topics at the bottom of page 553, you might send students out to the library—or to their computers—to actually look for a few sources. How many do they find? What were the best searching strategies for finding useful information? What dead ends did they come across? How do Internet sources compare to the library sources (in quality and quantity)?

How to plan research

Like the charts in Part Two that gave an overview of the writing process, this chart and others in this section are not intended to represent exactly how a research project progresses. Rather, research, like the rest of writing, is a recursive practice. Students may well have to back up and start some elements of their research over again before they find everything they need.

162

Student writer George Abukar's thesis evolves from a general topic area to a question to a claim. What he discovers through research persuades him that a particular claim is warranted. Now, his task is to use that research, and his own reasoning process, to persuade others to feel the same way.

Chapter Sixteen: Exploring Libraries

Be sure to access the resources available at *MyCompLab* go to (www.mycomplab.com and choose Faigley, *Writing: A Guide to College and Beyond*) to find helpful resources including Research Navigator as well as extensive instruction and activities for evaluating sources and avoiding plagiarism.

Chapter goals: Libraries are in many ways the heart of a college or university, and yet, a surprising number of students don't really know their way around one. This chapter gives students a sense of the kinds of information available in libraries, how it is organized, and how they can use it for their projects.

Chapter challenges: The sheer size of some college libraries is daunting to students, and can hinder their effective exploration. Moreover, the ease of Internet searches has led many to believe that everything they need to know can be found online. A few real research projects will often cure this misconception, as students are forced to look beyond Google and Yahoo for the sources they need.

There are two extremely valuable things you can do to drive home this chapter's lesson: bring a librarian in to your class, for a presentation or just a chat, and physically take your class to the library with you. Many schools have library staff that will be happy to set up a class visit; often, you can schedule an orientation session in the library for your students. Talking with an actual librarian can do much to demystify the library system for students. They may also be impressed by the amount of information librarians have at their fingertips—and therefore more willing to ask them for guidance in their research. And simply walking through the doors for the first time can make all the difference in how intimidating students find their campus library.

Determine the print sources you need
These are excellent questions for students to think about before they even head to the library. If you can discuss them in class after they have chosen topics for a research paper, so much the better. And remind your students that answers to these questions will help a librarian guide them toward helpful resources in the library.

Search using keywords
Even with the list of questions provided on page 557, students will often need help with keyword searches. To give you a sense of the habits they likely brought to college with them: the majority of keyword searches performed online consist of only one word. Combining keywords is a strategy they may have to learn.

Note that many online databases available in libraries now have advanced search features like those detailed for online searches in Chapter 18.

Find books

Encourage students to physically browse the shelves to get a better understanding of subject areas and possibilities. Although search engines can deliver thousands of "hits," they rarely display more than 10 or 20 sources per screen. There is just no substitute for walking down an aisle of books and letting the eye skim individual titles and groups of titles. Researchers who do this not only find sources they might never have located otherwise, they also gain a better understanding of how the scholarship in a given field is categorized and arranged by experts in that field.

Find journal articles

Note that there are usually two levels of searching required to find a journal article. If students locate an article title first, they must then often search for the journal itself by title, to locate it in the library. Or, students can locate likely journals and then search within them for individual articles. Encourage them, too, to flip through entire volumes and back issues for more information on their topic and the field.

To show students the difference between the various journal types, and the different ways they can be located, you might have them each pick a topic (or assign several from among which they can choose). Ask each student to bring in an article on that topic from a scholarly, a trade, and a popular journal. Have them summarize briefly what each of their articles does. Then, as a class, compare how each journal type treats its subject.

Evaluate print sources

It helps if you can provide students with a few scenarios where the importance of the questions on page 562 is clear. For example, how credible would you consider a book on global warming to be if it were published by:

- An internationally recognized university press?

- A publisher of popular bestsellers?

- A small press dedicated to environmental issues?

- A think-tank funded by oil companies?

- a private, "self-publishing" company, hired by the author?

You can also ask students to evaluate their own writing with the questions on 562—especially those questions concerning qualifications, evidence, and biases. This is an effective tactic during the drafting and revision stage.

Start a working bibliography

As we have already stressed repeatedly when referring to working theses, students should begin their working bibliographies with the expectation that they will evolve (not just grow). One important point that may help motivate students to keep a working bibliography (you can also require them to turn one in at some stage of the writing process—a good way to platform the research component of an assignment) is to remind them that they don't have to arrange all the information in perfect citation style as they go. If they prefer, they can do that detail work later, when they are certain which sources they will be using. What they must not do is fail to collect the information in the first place. There is no more frustrating way to spend research time than by looking up sources you already have but do not have the correct citation information for.

How to explore libraries

Like the charts in Part Two that give an overview of the writing process for various aims, this chart and others in this section are not intended to represent exactly how a research project progresses. Rather, research, like the rest of writing, is a recursive practice. Students may well have to back up and start some elements of their research over again before they find everything they need.

Chapter Seventeen: Online Libraries

> Be sure to access the resources available at *MyCompLab* go to
> (www.mycomplab.com and choose Faigley, *Writing: A Guide to College and Beyond*) to find helpful resources including Research Navigator as well as extensive instruction and activities for evaluating sources and avoiding plagiarism.

Chapter goals: In this chapter, students will learn about a resource that combines elements of two information sources they are probably already familiar with: libraries and electronic data searches.

Chapter challenges: Students may have trouble seeing, at first, how library databases are different from the Internet. They may also experience some confusion due to the multiplicity of databases available to them. Fortunately, most library Web sites offer excellent guidance in the use of the systems they subscribe to.

Note that we discuss some aspects of database searches previously in Chapter 16, in the section on journal articles.

Find information in databases

Electronic databases help reduce the sometimes time-consuming legwork inside libraries by allowing researchers to overview topic areas quickly, and hone in on specific sources accurately. Talk to a librarian at your institution about the databases available to your students. Some questions you might want to ask:

- How do the databases offered differ?

- How do you use them?

- For what subjects or type of research is each typically used?

- What features (e-mail citations, whole-text, printer-ready format, etc.) are available with each?

Construct effective searches

You want your students to understand the importance of trial and error as they search. When students begin searching a database, it is good for them to have a list of potential keywords ready, but students should also plan to modify that list as they go. In a networked classroom, you might do a search or two online, demonstrating for students how to select a database, try out various keywords and keyword combinations, and evaluate results (you can even try one out before class to see if it is likely to be instructive). This will model the entire process of inquiry for them—a valuable experience.

Remind your students that if they don't get good results from their first efforts at searching, they can ask for help. If they are able to explain to a reference librarian exactly how they have been searching, they'll get even more effective help—so encourage them to keep track of the search terms they try, and where they try them. Every database is different, but if your students keep trying, you can assure them that they'll eventually get the hang of it.

Locate elements of citation

Many databases will now send articles with complete bibliographic citations to any e-mail address the searcher supplies. Still, you should show your class where this information is located on a source in a typical database, so they don't become too reliant on these kinds of features.

Working Together: **Compare databases**

The last question in the series at the bottom of page 569 is the most important: Which items will be most helpful for a student's research project?

Students often need to get away from the idea that quantity equals quality. Research is where they really have to begin evaluating, choosing, and filtering. They have to narrow gradually, though, as they skim and read. A researcher shouldn't count on getting lucky and picking the best possible source from the first three she finds, because when she begins searching, she doesn't really know much about her topic yet.

How to explore online libraries

Like the charts in Part Two that give an overview of the writing process for various aims, the chart on page 570, and others in this section, are not intended to represent exactly how a research project progresses. Rather, research, like the rest of writing, is a recursive practice. Students may well have to back up and start some elements of their research over again before they find everything they need.

Researcher at Work: **Identifying useful articles in databases**

If your school has Business Source Premiere, you might try duplicating student writer George Abukar's search. Since BSP, like many databases, supplies results based in part on timeliness of sources, you may find that the results returned to you differ from the results George obtained. If your search yields different results, how do the sources you obtain differ from those obtained by George?

Chapter Eighteen: Exploring the Web

> Be sure to access the resources available at *MyCompLab* go to (www.mycomplab.com and choose Faigley, *Writing: A Guide to College and Beyond*) to find helpful resources including Research Navigator as well as extensive instruction and activities for evaluating sources and avoiding plagiarism.

Chapter goals: Students will hopefully come away from this chapter with a much broader view of what is available online, as well as a sense of healthy skepticism about the quality of information they may find there.

Chapter challenges: Some students may feel they already know everything there is to know about the Internet. They may need a little motivation before they are willing to try the specific search methods outlined here. On the other hand, even today you may have students who are not at all familiar with the Internet and are less than eager to learn about it. Usually, the exposure of the latter group to the former helps alleviate this problem: students are often eager to learn knowledge they see their classmates have already mastered and put to good use.

Find information on the Web

Ask your students which search engines they use most frequently, and why. You might also ask what kinds of documents they've found online (forms, articles, reviews, items to purchase, PDFs, word documents, MP3 files, etc.) through Web searches. Showing your class what they already know is a nice way to engage them in the process of learning even more.

Evaluate Web sources

A good exercise to show your class the value of the criteria on page 576 is to ask them about any documents they've found online that weren't what they initially seemed to be. Given the amount of time the typical college student spends online today, they have all probably had this experience at least once. Ask them some of the following questions, and discuss with the class:

- What did the page initially seem to be?

- What did it turn out to be?

- How did you eventually figure out the site was misleading?

- How did you feel about the authors of the information after you made this discovery?

Find visual sources online

Those of your students who aren't familiar with image searching will probably pick it up quite quickly. The larger issue where online images are concerned is copyright. Its abuse is rampant and becoming ever more problematic.

One way you might demonstrate the seriousness of image "borrowing" is to have your students bring in files of a few digital photos they've taken themselves. Warn them that other students will be working with the photos. Have students exchange files (they might just be able to post them to a course Web site) and then let their peers download the photos and manipulate them, using Photoshop or another graphics program. What does it feel like to see one's own work appropriated by another person? If a perfect stranger did this with an image they posted online, how would they feel? How would they feel if the resulting, manipulated image was sold for a lot of money?

Write Now: **Evaluate Web sites**

After students have chosen a hoax for the exercise on the bottom of page 577, and evaluated a specific hoax Web site, ask them to do a general search for references to the hoax across the Internet. In what sources is it recognized or not recognized as a hoax?

How to explore the Web

Like the charts in Part Two that give an overview of the writing process for various aims, this chart and others in this section are not intended to represent exactly how a research project progresses. Rather, research, like the rest of writing, is a recursive practice. Students may well have to back up and start some elements of their research over again before they find everything they need.

Researcher at Work: **Identifying useful sources online**

As with the BSP database search discussed above, your students can try George Abukar's search on Google and note how the results have changed over time. Remind them that Google and many other search engines privilege pages that are more recent and have been recently accruing the most hits. Ask them to think about how "recent interest" correlates with "value of content."

Chapter Nineteen: Exploring in the Field

> Be sure to access the resources available at *MyCompLab* go to
> (www.mycomplab.com and choose Faigley, *Writing: A Guide to College and
> Beyond*) to find helpful resources including Research Navigator as well as
> extensive instruction and activities for evaluating sources and avoiding plagiarism.

Chapter goals: Primary research is a critical college skill, and there is little point in waiting until a student's final year in college to expose him or her to it. This chapter will show students the basics of conducting primary research, as well as give them an idea of its value.

Chapter challenges: As hard as it is for some students to get to the library, conducting primary research is harder still. They may be intimidated by the planning required, or simply nervous about making direct contact with strangers. If you require primary research for a paper, try to give students some options that do not force them into awkward social settings (unless, of course, you are teaching a methods course where interviewing and surveying are part of the curriculum).

We strongly advise you to check with your institution's Human Subjects Review Board before students begin any research. Usually, undergraduate research will be exempt from most controls, but sometimes students will need approval for their projects. Regardless, it's good for students to see how human subjects research is monitored and approved at institutions of higher learning. And it's very important for you, as the instructor, to set the example by following your school's research protocol.

Conduct interviews

Likewise, if you *require* interviews, give your students some basic safety rules to follow as they schedule and conduct them: don't put yourself in awkward or dangerous, illegal situations; make appointments in advance, get permission for surveys, etc. These strategies may seem obvious to you, but you don't want to put young, inexperienced people at risk based on what you assume they should already know.

You will greatly increase your students' chances of conducting successful interviews if you give them an idea of where to go for subjects, or perhaps even a pre-screened pool of professors or others willing to be interviewed. This tactic keeps shy students from being at too much of a disadvantage.

Administer surveys

Keep tabs on your students' surveying efforts (for one thing, make sure they aren't waiting until the last minute to conduct them). Remind them when necessary of the need to get permission to take surveys in certain locations, and of the need to not irritate potential survey-takers with their requests.

When surveys are completed, your students may need additional information on how to interpret the results. Hopefully, they will have thought about this issue as they designed the survey. But unexpected results may complicate their research process and require some re-thinking of their approach or their thesis.

Make observations

Of course, it would be ideal if students chose research methods based entirely upon what would provide the best information for their project. However, if your goal is simply to give students some experience with primary research, observation can be an ideal research choice for students who shy away from interviewing and surveying.

The section of this resource manual that discusses Chapter 8 contains a wealth of additional information on teaching students to use observations.

Write Now: **Compose interview questions**

After students write the interview questions suggested in the activity at the bottom of page 585, have them exchange their lists of questions, read them, and then suggest additional questions their peer might consider asking.

How to conduct field research

Like the charts in Part Two that give an overview of the writing process for various aims, the chart on page 586, and others in this section, are not intended to represent exactly how a research project progresses. Rather, research, like the rest of writing, is a recursive practice. Students may well have to back up and start some elements of their research over again before they find everything they need.

Researcher at Work: **Designing a survey**

Have your students consider the *limitations* of student writer George Abukar's survey. How representative is his sample? Are there other questions he could have asked? Would your students have stopped to take the survey? Why or why not?

Overall, do your students think his is the best possible survey George Abukar could have conducted for his research purposes? What would they have done differently, if anything?

Chapter Twenty: Writing the Research Paper

> Be sure to access the resources available at *MyCompLab* go to
> (www.mycomplab.com and choose Faigley, *Writing: A Guide to College and
> Beyond*) to find helpful resources including Research Navigator as well as
> extensive instruction and activities for evaluating sources and avoiding plagiarism.

Chapter goals: Using this chapter in conjunction with relevant chapters in Part Two, students should be able to write a well-organized and readable research paper, free of plagiarism.

Chapter challenges: As the preceding chapters have made clear, the writing of a research paper requires combining numerous tasks. Even if they have excelled at all the previous components, students may feel intimidated and overwhelmed when they sit down to begin drafting. They may have trouble starting, or they may rush through their draft, feeling that the writing is less important than the research itself.

Plan your organization

Of course, the organization of a paper can change as a writer proceeds through drafts. But with any paper, it helps to begin with a plan. Because of the added complexity of research papers, this is especially true. Before they sit down to write, your students should take some time to reconsider their thesis in light of all the work they have done so far.

It can be hard for any writer to determine exactly what he or she is contributing to a discourse. Student writers especially are apt to have trouble seeing how their paper will do more than simply report existing knowledge. The list of questions on page 589 will help them firm up their sense of what they have done that is new. You might also take these questions into consideration when designing research assignments—they may help you better describe your expectations for the assignment.

Avoid plagiarism

In general, a writer (and especially a student writer) is better off citing too often than not enough. As they revise and edit their drafts, students can change more quotations to paraphrases, and integrate quotes more smoothly. But if they are at all uncertain about their manipulation of quoted material, you can encourage them to begin by quoting and citing every source in their initial draft. Then, provided they edit carefully, they will avoid any potential problems with plagiarism.

See the first part of this resource manual for general information about avoiding plagiarism in the writing classroom. The penalties for plagiarism should be outlined for students at the beginning of the semester. At the very least, remind students that if they have any doubt or uncertainty about how to handle a source, they should alert you to the problem before turning in their draft. That way you will know, if there is a problem, that the student is making an honest effort to cite correctly.

Quote sources without plagiarizing

You might task students with trying this quoting and paraphrasing exercise themselves, using sources relevant to their paper. This is one good way to "platform" the process of incorporating quotations, especially for less experienced students. Once you and they are certain they can manage a few quotes on their own, they can work through the rest of their draft more confidently.

Summarize and paraphrase sources without plagiarizing

Summarized and paraphrased sources, especially in combination with direct quotation, give a paper valuable contrast, and help greatly with readability. It is somewhat trickier than direct quotation, calling for a certain amount of good judgment, and your students will probably need help developing this.

Incorporate quotations

It takes a while for writers to develop a sense of the back-and-forth feeling a good research paper presents to readers. The author's voice should control the conversation, but quotation of outside sources provides support and counter-argument. This gives readers the sense of witnessing a conversation rather than a lecture. To show your students the effect of this important writing technique, you might consider showing them a passage from a research paper that has had all the quotations stripped out, leaving only the author's voice. How effective is the author's argument without the other voices?

Incorporate visuals

Before they understand *how* to use visuals, students need to know *why* they are using them. Your assignment sheet should make clear to students the purpose of any required visuals. You and your students can refer to Part Four of *Writing: A Guide for College and Beyond* for more in-depth information about visual design.

Try to work especially closely with any students who will be creating visuals from data they have collected. It is easy for even an honest researcher to produce charts and graphs that skew data. As an example, you can ask them to look at the charts on page 629, showing the survey information gathered by student writer George Abukar. The same information is represented in table form on page 587.

Finally, students may have trouble writing captions for their visuals. Explain to them that a great visual, poorly labeled, can do more harm than good in a paper.

Write Now: **Summarize, paraphrase, and quote directly**

After your students complete the activity at the bottom of page 598, have them compare their summaries, paraphrases, and incorporated quotations. The class as a whole can check each one for accuracy, and at the same time see the many different ways of doing each task correctly.

Review your research project

The instructions and suggestions on page 599 make an excellent peer review format. Students can also use it on their own papers as well. You might base your own comments on rough drafts on the questions listed here.

How to write a research paper

Like the charts in Part Two that give an overview of the writing process for various aims, this chart and others in this section are not intended to represent exactly how a research project progresses. Rather, research, like the rest of writing, is a recursive practice. Students may well have to back up and start some elements of their research over again before they find everything they need.

Researcher at Work: **Varying quotations, summaries, and paraphrases**

Ask your students why they think George Abukar chose to include the lengthy quote from the FTC Web site. What is its effect on readers? What point does it make for the author?

Sometimes a long quotation is needed to accurately convey a complex point. Sometimes long quotes can be used to give readers a sense of the original author or speaker's tone or style. Here, the lengthy set of instructions for consumers helps George Abukar make his point that the instructions are too exhaustive to be of any real help.

Chapter Twenty-one: MLA Documentation

> Be sure to access the resources available at *MyCompLab* go to
> (www.mycomplab.com and choose Faigley, *Writing: A Guide to College and Beyond*) to find helpful resources including Research Navigator as well as extensive instruction and activities for evaluating sources and avoiding plagiarism.

Chapter goals: Students should learn from this chapter that MLA documentation style is no great mystery, but rather a set of detailed rules that can be followed easily once the writer understands their purpose. They should see that the bulk of this chapter is a reference they can use to format their MLA-style papers properly.

Chapter challenges: For some reason, it is occasionally hard to impress upon students that both parts of MLA documentation—in-text citation and the Works Cited list—are equally important. Then too, it may take one or two papers before students really understand that proper citation is a part of their grade, and not just a finishing touch on par with a handsome presentation folder. It's wise to warn them in advance what will happen to their grade if they do not use proper documentation style.

Elements of MLA documentation

MLA-style documentation, like APA style, involves in-text and end-of-text information. Ask your students if they have ever followed up an in-text citation to find out more about the source. If they haven't, encourage them to try this the next time they are reading a text with citations.

Remind students that footnotes, though they frequently appear in MLA-style papers, are not themselves a component of MLA documentation.

Entries in the Works Cited list

Oddly enough, the most frequent error in students' Works Cited list (apart from failing to include one entirely) is the failure to alphabetize. Point out to your class that this section of the chapter describes the types of entries according to how common they are. But they should not list their Works Cited entries in this order (books, then periodicals, then online sources, etc.).

In-text citations in MLA style

The samples included here will cover most of the sources your students are likely to use. However, they may need to refer to the MLA handbook (you can bring one from the library to show them if necessary) for entries not listed here. Citation methods for Web sources, in particular, can change frequently.

If you wish, you may refer students to this section by page or entry number as you review drafts and comment on their citation.

Sample MLA paper

Beginning on page 624, student writer George Abukar's lengthy research and writing process, mapped out in the preceding chapters of this part of *Writing: A Guide for College and Beyond*, culminates in the full, final version of his paper. You and your students might refer to this paper to clarify many questions about MLA-style research papers.

Chapter Twenty-two: APA Documentation

> Be sure to access the resources available at **MyCompLab** go to (www.mycomplab.com and choose Faigley, *Writing: A Guide to College and Beyond*) to find helpful resources including Research Navigator as well as extensive instruction and activities for evaluating sources and avoiding plagiarism.

Chapter goals: Students should learn from this chapter that APA documentation style is no great mystery, but rather a set of detailed rules that can be followed easily once the writer understands their purpose. They should see that the bulk of this chapter is a reference they can use to format their APA-style papers properly.

Chapter challenges: For some reason it is occasionally hard to impress upon students that both parts of APA documentation—in-text citation and the References page—are equally important. Then too, it may take one or two papers before students really understand that proper citation is a part of their grade, and not just a finishing touch on par with a handsome presentation folder. It's wise to warn them in advance what will happen to their grade if they do not use proper documentation style.

APA citations

APA-style documentation, like MLA style, involves in-text and end-of-text information. Ask your students if they have ever followed up an in-text citation to find out more about the source. If they haven't, encourage them to try this the next time they are reading a text with citations.

Remind students that footnotes, though they frequently appear in APA-style papers, are not themselves a component of APA documentation.

In-text citations in APA style

The samples included here will cover most of the sources your students are likely to use. However, they may need to refer to an APA handbook (you can bring one from the library to show them if necessary) for entries not listed here. Citation methods for Web sources, in particular, can change frequently.

If you wish, you may refer students to this section by page or entry number as you review drafts and comment on their citation.

Reference lists in APA style

Oddly enough, the most frequent error in students' References pages (apart from failing to include one entirely) is the failure to alphabetize. Point out to your class that this section of the chapter describes the types of entries according to how common they are. But they should not list their References page entries in this order (books, then periodicals, then online sources, etc.).

Sample APA paper
Beginning on page 647, students can read a research review written in APA style. You and your students might refer to this paper to clarify many questions about APA-style research papers.

PART FOUR: THE WRITER AS DESIGNER

Teaching design and collaboration skills for writers

Today's students have, for the most part, lived lives saturated with visual stimuli. Most of them spend a great deal of time on the Internet, and can critique Web site design very competently. They know a great deal about how images work, but they may not be aware of how to use what they know effectively. Integrating visuals with writing may also prove challenging for them— just as it is challenging for professional writers.

In the past, writers and designers usually collaborated on projects with visual elements. While this kind of collaboration is still common, the proliferation of desktop publishing technologies gives every writer with a computer the ability to add sophisticated images to his or her work. More and more, writers are not just able, but expected, to do so. Understanding visual design can make images a real asset to writing, not just window dressing.

We are also expected, in today's professional world, to deliver effective presentations, with appropriate verbal and visual elements. Even when a presentation software application promises to give our work all the structure it needs, writers must still understand what makes an effective presentation.

In the work world, much, if not most, writing is produced collaboratively. Team-written documents are increasingly common in college classes as a result, and students should learn early in their college careers how to productively handle an assignment when working in a group.

All these valuable real-world skills are covered in Part Four of *Writing: A Guide for College and Beyond*.

Chapter Twenty-three: Thinking Visually

Be sure to access the resources available at *MyCompLab* go to (www.mycomplab.com and choose Faigley, *Writing: A Guide to College and Beyond*) to find additional resources for writing, design help and using visuals.

Chapter goals: This chapter will help you and your students develop some vocabulary for talking about images. Students will also see what effective visuals look like, and why they work.

Chapter challenges: Even when students see the value of learning about visual design, they may have trouble articulating words and phrases to accurately describe what visuals are trying to convey (after all, "a picture is worth a thousand words"). Yet the struggle to pin down visual nuance helps students then reverse the process, creating or selecting images that accurately represent the subtleties of what they are trying to say with words. Moreover, working to more precisely describe what they see improves students' overall vocabulary.

Communicate with visuals and words

This chapter (and indeed this whole part) of *Writing: A Guide for College and Beyond* is designed to be taught in conjunction with a specific project where students will be likely to use visuals. This allows them to think about the concepts in the chapter in the context of their own work. A few students, such as those who have a background or interest in design or art, may already be quite familiar with this chapter's ideas. But the combining of words and images is a skill they will probably all need to practice, regardless of past experience.

Take care when constructing assignments that require visuals. If the visual elements are not truly needed to accomplish the assignment's aim, you will only teach students how to use visuals as a distraction from their words.

Understand visual and verbal concepts

When you discuss this section in class, you might ask your students to each choose one image in the chapter and describe it in a brief, informal piece of writing. Ask them to search for words that describe the emphasis, balance, contrast, repetition, point of view, motion, or detail they see in the image. Then, have each description read aloud. Compare the elements described and the language used (this would be a great activity for the instructor to do along with the class).

Chapter Twenty-four: Creating Visuals

> Be sure to access the resources available at *MyCompLab* go to
> (www.mycomplab.com and choose Faigley, *Writing: A Guide to College and Beyond*) to find additional resources for writing, design help and using visuals.

Chapter goals: This chapter aims to show students the difference between indifferent and powerful images, and suggests strategies to use to create powerful images.

Chapter challenges: The advent of digital photography has made it much easier to use trial and error when taking photographs. Therefore, the greatest challenge for students in this chapter centers not on photography but on the accurate production of tables, charts, and graphs (page 667). Many of us become overly reliant on software to produce effective graphics from data, without stopping to consider if the charts produced really meet our needs (and our readers') as well as they could.

Know when to use images and graphics

To illustrate the point in this section, try to find, or have students look for, a few examples of inappropriately used images—they are not too hard to find on the Web and in advertisements. Distinguish between distracting or misleading images and the kind of associative fallacies often found in advertising (e.g., the slinky model on top of the car being advertised). Poor image choice as we are discussing it here means an image that counteracts the writing's intended message or purpose.

Ask your students about their personal experience with graphics—software programs, drawing, sign-making, and related skills: Photoshop, uploading images to the Web, animation, font manipulation and WordArt, digital and traditional photography, drawing, etc. You probably have at least a couple of experts on hand right in your classroom. Consider having these students do a mini-tutorial for the whole class on their skills, in the context of one paper or project.

Emerging technologies like YouTube mean that video is now also a potential accompaniment to writing, at least online. Ask students how they have seen, or tried themselves to "write around" video.

Take pictures that aren't boring

If your students have access to cameras, an interesting exercise might be to send them all out to photograph a single subject, then compare and discuss the results. They could perhaps turn in three images each, with a written description of their composition process, editing choices, and the final products. What do they think each image conveys? What techniques did their classmates try that hadn't occurred to them?

If your students don't have access to cameras, you could recast this activity by having them look at as many images as possible of some landmark, such as the Statue of Liberty, Mount Rushmore, the White House, or the Empire State building. What choices did each photographer make while composing the image? What do your students think the photographer was trying to convey?

Compose images

Just as writers must compose their thoughts in a way that makes sense to readers, and edit their words for clarity, images should be thoughtfully composed and edited so that only the essential information remains. With visuals, the composition process is much more compressed than it is with writing (which can be manipulated indefinitely). Thus, it's a good idea to take multiple photographs of a subject, or create a range of thumbnail charts, and then work with the range of options available in the series of images before choosing the final version.

Edit images

Images can also (and often are, albeit sometimes inadvertently) manipulated and skewed. Proportions can be altered, surfaces smoothed, lightened, darkened. People can be made to look thinner, fatter, older, or less wrinkled than they really are. Talk about the ethical implications of this process—it is endemic on magazine covers, especially with images of women.

You might ask your students to think about the ethics of composing images: at what point does it become "dishonest" to manipulate an image? In what contexts is it acceptable or not acceptable? Is enhancing a photograph of a person any different from that person wearing makeup while being photographed? You can also have your students look for some stories in the news about unethical or questionable photo manipulation. This topic is currently being debated in the public sphere as technologies make it easier for images to reflect an ideal rather than reality. And, if your students are tempted to skew any of their own visuals, point out to them that as more and more people become conversant with the technologies, more and more dishonest uses of it are likely to be discovered.

Create tables, charts, and graphs

Strongly caution your students against "prettying up" charts and data. An inaccurate or misleading chart can undo hours or even years of careful research and writing. Moreover, skewed charts give a distinct impression of bias on the part of the writer.

Many elements we are used to seeing in popular graphics are unnecessary and could actually interfere with our comprehension of the data presented. Designer Edward Tufte (see his essay "PowerPoint is Evil" in Part Two of *Writing: A Guide for College and Beyond*) refers to these unneeded elements as "clutter."

Three-dimensional charts, for example, are often clutter. Too often, the third dimension does not convey any information. Too many colors are clutter—if you only have two classifications, use two colors, or even black and white. Remind your class that just because an application like Excel gives them the capability to add cool-looking features doesn't mean those features will make their charts better, easier to read, or more accurate. The reverse in fact is usually true. You

190

might set them the task of turning a single data set into five or more chart styles, to see which does the best job of accurately conveying the information.

Working Together

You can make the activity on page 667 even more challenging by presenting students with a complex chart or graph and asking them to reproduce it verbally. How much detail can they provide, compared to the graphic, without overwhelming readers?

They may find themselves resorting to visual imagery in their prose as they do this—a good indicator of how strongly humans rely on visual organization to process complex information.

Chapter Twenty-five: Designing for Print

> Be sure to access the resources available at *MyCompLab* go to
> (www.mycomplab.com and choose Faigley, *Writing: A Guide to College and Beyond*) to find additional resources for writing, design help and using visuals.

Chapter goals: In this chapter students will get a sense of how print conventions can be controlled to enhance a reader's journey through the text.

Chapter challenges: Students are often so used to formatting papers according to guidelines from instructors that it may never have occurred to them to control these variables for the purpose of enhancing their writing. They need to get used to seeing their own writing as a viable product that can and should resemble other well-formatted writing they see, and not just a standardized document designed to meet basic standards.

Discuss the images on the opening page with your students. What is off-putting or, in the language of the caption, not truthful about the third images? Have students articulate the way the images make them feel—words like "closed," "unfriendly," "hard," "daunting," and "hostile" might come up.

Start with your readers

Remember that students usually need explicit instruction and explanation of the structure they are learning to use—reports, headings, etc. They can't make their paper's organization visible to readers if they don't know what their readers expect, or why. Often, students graduate and enter a field without ever fully learning that field's writing format, because no one ever explains to them the reason for its features. Why, for example, does a business report have an executive summary? Because the CEO only has 90 seconds to spend reading it!

If you don't know the reason for features of a form you are teaching, find out as much as you can about it. The explanation "There's no real reason; that's just the way it's done in Marketing (Biology, Engineering, etc.)" is not only unhelpful to students trying to master the form—it's also rarely true.

Use headings and subheadings effectively

Caution students against the overuse of headings. Yes, they are a convenient way to stretch out a paper to meet a minimum page length, but that doesn't make them helpful to the reader. To demonstrate, bring in a long document with a lot of headings (you could, for example, download a PDF of a report from the Web site of the Government Accountability Office) and have students read only the headings. How much does this tell them about the document as a whole?

Design pages

If you regularly give students basic style guidelines for their papers, you might refer to the advice in this section in your paper assignment sheets, or even in your syllabus, if you wish.

Again, you should probably caution students against over-using white space to meet minimum page requirements. This may be tempting in college, but it looks painfully obvious. When students begin writing for their jobs after college, they will all too often find that meeting minimum lengths is not the problem—that being concise is the most important quality of any writing they produce. White space should therefore only be used as needed to provide structure.

Understand typography

A fun way to expose students to more varieties of font than they have typically used is to give them, or have them provide, a short passage in a word processing document. Ask them put it into five to 10 different fonts. Then have them write short descriptions of how each text block looks: serious, business-like, formal, informal, easy to read, hard to read, etc. They should think about both first impressions and ease of use.

Among other things, this exercise should show them that fonts look different in larger blocks than in the few words they see when choosing a font. You might also break up the entire font list available on classroom computers and distribute them among your class. Working with the same passage, have each student put it into three or five of the fonts on the list, and then compare them all. This will give students a better sense of the full range of font options available to them.

Since some students may not be familiar with it, demonstrate and explain the View or Zoom feature that most word processing applications have. Note that the font that they see onscreen isn't necessarily the same as what will come off the printer.

Advise your students to bookmark the checklist on page 675; they can refer back to it when they are drafting and revising papers.

Write Now: **Design a menu**

After designing the menus described on page 675, students can turn them in to you, or exchange them, for feedback. It is wise to double-check the sources of any images they use. They may be tempted to use copyrighted images without permission.

Note that if students don't have access to color printing (it's getting cheaper, but you still can't assume everyone has it or can afford it), they must choose images that work well in black and white. Sharp contrast and focus may need more consideration in this case.

Remind students too that, for printed documents, your images are only as good as your printer!

Write Now: **Create a brochure**

The activity on pages 676-677, like the preceding activity involving menus, gives students a great chance to look over and critique one another's work. When all the brochures are completed, display them on a table and let students browse through them. Ask them what design features they notice first among the brochures. Which one presents its information most clearly? Which is most striking? Which is the most fun to read?

As noted above, you should keep in mind with projects like this that not all students will have equal access to printing resources. Black and white and poorer quality printers can still be used to produce effective documents, but students working with these narrower parameters will have different design decisions to make. This often calls for great ingenuity and even more careful planning.

Chapter Twenty-six: Designing a Web Site

Be sure to access the resources available at **MyCompLab** go to (www.mycomplab.com and choose Faigley, *Writing: A Guide to College and Beyond*) to find additional resources for writing, design help and using visuals.

Chapter goals: Though students probably feel they know a good or bad Web site when they see one, they may not have thought much about the thought and effort that goes into creating a good Web site. This chapter will help them through the process if Web site design is a requirement or option in your course.

Chapter challenges: Finding the optimum balance between visuals and text is hard even for professional Web designers. Students will need to think about audience, and re-evaluate their site as they work on it, to make sure it is readable, navigable, and attractive to viewers.

Plan a Web site

While publication to the World Wide Web gives anyone in the world access to your work (provided they have an Internet connection), you can't think of the whole world as your audience. Students might begin by asking how their audience is likely to find their site in the first place. Will they already be interested in the subject when they get there? How much background information will they need?

Sometimes the best way to understand good design is to note its absence. You might try finding a few Web pages that are especially poorly designed, and discussing their features with your class.

Make your site visually effective

Help your students identify the "visual theme" for a few good Web sites, and they will quickly get a sense of what they should strive for in their own designs. They probably have some sites that they already think of as visually effective. Try looking at these as a class, using some of the language for visual elements covered earlier in Chapter 23. Look specifically at elements like text, color, headings, links, and background.

Write Now: **Evaluate a Web site**

Students can compare the first evaluation they do for the activity on page 680 with a second one, created after following a link other than Students or Current Students. How are parents, alumni, or faculty, for example, guided through your school's Web site? How did the designers seem to think they would use the site? What information is provided for them that is not highlighted for students? And vice versa?

Make navigation easy

Have students find four or five examples of different navigation bars on Web sites. Ask them to compare their placement, size, number of buttons and tabs, and the overall usability of the navigational system. Which navigation systems work best for them, and why?

The checklist for evaluating Web sites is a handy resource to come back to when students are designing their sites or reviewing one another's Web designs. If you are grading Web projects, you might want to take the criteria here into consideration when designing the assignment and grading sheets.

Chapter Twenty-seven: Delivering Presentations

Be sure to access the resources available at *MyCompLab* go to (www.mycomplab.com and choose Faigley, *Writing: A Guide to College and Beyond*) to find additional resources for writing, design help and using visuals.

Chapter goals: Students should learn from this chapter how to organize ideas into a presentation format that will be coherent to audiences. They will also learn to avoid some of the more common pitfalls of presentations.

Chapter challenges: Apart from the reticence to speak before groups that is common among many people, students may face additional challenges. They may be overuse presentation software, and decline to interrogate its real contribution to their presentation. Or, they may find oral presentation so painful that they rush through their talk as quickly as possible, without giving their project the delivery it deserves.

Plan a presentation

Students should be given some sense, in the assignment, of *why* they are presenting instead of communicating information in some other format. Why are presentations used in the workplace? Ask students to think of situations in the work world where they may need to present: pitching a campaign or product to clients, reporting to employers, etc.

There are key differences in audience expectations for presentations and for papers or reports, and key differences in the way the information is received. For one thing, it is very different to have the audience in front of you—in fact, this is a luxury writers don't have, so students should be advised to take advantage of it. They need to be ready to adjust and adapt as they present, because—unlike the writer of a report—they can.

Give a memorable presentation

Ask students to recall good, bad, and painful presentations they have sat through. What qualities can they duplicate or avoid themselves?

You can use the list of qualities on page 685 to evaluate presentations your students do, and when students evaluate their peers' presentations.

Write Now: **Moving across media**

You might have students do the activity on the bottom of page 685 first with, and then without, using presentation software. Then ask them: Which was easier? Which do they think an audience would probably prefer?

Chapter Twenty-eight: Working as a Team

> Be sure to access the resources available at **MyCompLab** go to (www.mycomplab.com and choose Faigley, *Writing: A Guide to College and Beyond*) to find additional resources for writing, design help and using visuals.

Chapter goals: This chapter gives students some specific tools for managing team-writing situations. Students will learn about the dynamics of groups and how to stay focused on group goals.

Chapter challenges: Like everyone else, students have individual personalities that sometimes make group work frustrating or unproductive. With well-structured assignments from you, however, these difficulties can be minimized, making group work a valuable learning opportunity.

Organize a team

Be prepared to intervene and mentor your student groups. Random class groupings are rarely as cohesive and balanced as workplace groups, since your students will have varied stakes, motivation levels, time, and skills. Grouping students according to interest or topic often works well, though there will inevitably be a few students who aren't terribly interested in whatever topic they end up working on.

You might provide some organization options at the outset, building in a work plan, for example, as an early component of the larger project. Some instructors also require groups to name a Team Leader, Moderator, Recorder, or other offices, to fulfill specific roles. Give *explicit* directions if you want students to divide up tasks in certain ways.

Understand the team process

Look at the team process chart with your class and note how many ways there are for a single member to derail the process. Notice too, however, how much easier some steps, such as "create" and "evaluate" become, when you have a number of people actively engaged in them.

Work as a team

It's a good idea to build into group assignments some method for students to communicate directly to you about group dynamics in case of problems. A process log, for example, describing all the plans made by the group, and then the actual work done by each member, written directly to you and turned in twice—mid-project and end—will help keep everyone honest about their contributions.

Working Together: What to do when problems arise in teams

It wouldn't hurt to preview any group projects with the activity on the bottom of page 689. Stress also you are there as a backup in case students can't handle problems on their own.

You can also, if you like, let students vent a little at the beginning of the project, before the groups are arranged, about times when they have done group work in the past and felt they were taken advantage of. This is a none-too-subtle way of warning potential slackers how unpopular they will be with their classmates.

PART FIVE: THE WRITER AS EDITOR

Note: Chapters 29-33 appear only in the full hardcover version of *Writing: A Guide for College and Beyond*. They do not appear in the paperback "Brief" version of the text.

Every writer has a different style, and yet there are many stylistic factors that most good writing exhibits. Effective use of paragraphs to organize ideas, effective use of sentence structure, and freedom from mechanical error are all qualities that make readers feel writing is "good"— because these qualities help readers to follow the writer's ideas. This part of *Writing: A Guide for College and Beyond* sets a good example by explaining, concisely, how student writers can develop a reader-friendly style in their writing.

Much of the work of writing lies in re-writing, fine tuning, and polishing words. This part of the text will be especially useful to your students as they proceed onward from the rough draft stage. When they have their basic ideas on paper, but need to shape and clarify them, you can refer them to the chapters here that address paragraphs, sentences, and specific grammatical and punctuation errors.

Finally, Chapter 33 offers specific help for students who do not speak English as their first language.

On most pages of this section, you will find checklists of questions students can ask about their writing. These shorter lists are combined, in each chapter, into a single checklist which both you and your students can use when working to revise papers.

Each of these chapters illustrates its advice with examples from various texts. When working with your students on these concepts, however, it is critical that you discuss their own writing, not the work of other writers. Research shows that students learn mechanical aspects of writing, and retain the concepts longer, when they learn them in the context of their own work rather than in rote grammar exercises or by correcting others' mistakes. Students cannot learn "style" without learning *their own* style.

Chapter Twenty-nine: Writing Effective Paragraphs

> Be sure to access the resources available at *MyCompLab* go to (www.mycomplab.com and choose Faigley, *Writing: A Guide to College and Beyond*) to find extensive instruction and practice with grammar and mechanics, as well as ESL instruction and activities.

Chapter goals: Students need to see how paragraph structure guides readers' (and writers') comprehension of the material. In this chapter, students can see not just how good paragraphs help readers, but also how thinking about paragraph structure can help them as writers.

Chapter challenges: Students often think of paragraphs as little more than units of length, each containing one topic sentence and a certain amount of additional material. Showing them the logic underlying various patterns of paragraph organization should help move them past this overly simplistic approach to paragraphing.

Develop paragraphs

There is a difference, of course, between developing a paragraph with relevant information and padding it with extraneous material. It is at the paragraph level that you will most often see evidence of students' inability or unwillingness to engage in critical thinking. Thus, the paragraph is often the best place to push students to take their ideas further. Focusing on one or two paragraphs in a draft, and prodding the student to further develop their ideas, gives them a model for how to think throughout the paper.

Give them specific advice on their drafts about dividing, combining, and refocusing paragraphs. This is the kind of macro-structural change students often resist because it seems like too much work. They will need help seeing the possibilities and advantages of engaging in this sort of re-thinking.

Pay attention to paragraph length

In most classes, if you have students identify the longest paragraph in a draft they have written, they will find that they can easily subdivide it into two, three, or even four paragraphs. Have them try this exercise, and then ask them a few questions:

- How did they choose the dividing points?

- Were additional transitional devices needed or did some need to be removed?

- What is the effect after each division is made?

- How many paragraphs seem optimal?

Link within and across paragraphs

In their own work, students may have trouble distinguishing between repetition and redundancy. In the beginning it is usually better to be too repetitive than to risk confusing the reader. But as students develop their writing skills, they should be on the lookout for ways to reduce unneeded repetition that slows readers down.

There are many ways to organize paragraphs. The key to holding together an organizational pattern is to use the appropriate transitions. Words like "but," "yet," and "however" indicate contrast. "First, second, and third" are used for chronological or ordinal patterns. Terms like "closest, farther, most distant," indicate spatial relationships. Most students will be perfectly familiar with these transition words as vocabulary elements, but they may not think of them in clusters that help them organize their ideas. You might have your class assemble a list or lists of transitional words and phrases, and the circumstances for using each.

Start fast

Emphasize to students that they shouldn't panic if their first drafts are slow starters. If they worry too early about conciseness, their fluency may suffer and they won't sufficiently develop their ideas. Warn them not to get stuck trying to write a fast opening before they even draft their papers!

Conclude with strength

Conclusions are hard to write for any document, but especially in response to writing assignments, where they may seem artificial. Have your students try several of these strategies for one of their papers, and choose the one they think works best. They could do this just before or as they finalize their opening paragraphs. Bracketing the opening and closing elements of the papers this way allows students to think about the arc of their paper, and what it accomplishes.

Summary for editing paragraphs

The checklist on page 701 is an excellent reference for you and your students when revising and editing drafts. You can incorporate it into peer review, or refer to it yourself when giving students feedback on their drafts.

Chapter Thirty: Writing Effective Sentences

> Be sure to access the resources available at *MyCompLab* go to
> (www.mycomplab.com and choose Faigley, *Writing: A Guide to College and Beyond*) to find extensive instruction and practice with grammar and mechanics, as well as ESL instruction and activities.

Chapter goals: Students know the sentence as the basic structural unit of writing. This chapter gives them a new look at the options they have when building sentences, and how they can choose among those options to make their writing stronger.

Chapter challenges: Students may feel that if a sentence is "correct," with no glaring grammatical errors, there is no need to improve upon it. Taking sentences from "blah" to "effective" involves some work, but students need to understand how their work pays off in terms of audience reception.

Understand sentence basics

Most students will know that a sentence requires a subject and a verb, but reviewing these terms will help you when you want to discuss more complex aspects of their writing. It is the many possible relationships between subject and verb that tend to get writers into trouble at the sentence level. In particular, being able to effectively coordinate and subordinate ideas within sentences is key to writing well in college.

Especially in college, when they are beginning to write about more complex ideas than they have ever addressed before, students will find that their sentences become more complex too. To make these sentences hang together and work effectively, they will need to pay attention to all the techniques outlined in this chapter.

Pay attention to verbs

Sometimes it can be hard for a writer to think of alternate verbs. We get so focused on being precise with our meaning that it is difficult to "loosen up" again and search for more colorful language. One way to spark some of this energy in student papers is to have them exchange drafts at some point and suggest alternative verbs for their peers' papers. They can even use a thesaurus to help them with this task. Stress, though, that writers shouldn't sacrifice accuracy for the sake of color. How much does the meaning of a sentence change when a new verb is substituted for the old one?

Stay active

Students clearly have trouble identifying passive constructions, or they wouldn't use so many of them. This is one area of writing instruction where face-to-face interaction is often most valuable. Meeting with a student and pointing out each passive construction in a draft, and then having the student re-articulate the sentence with an active construction, can go a long way toward clearing up passive prose.

You can also ask students to bring in some examples of the passive voice from their research and reading. Is there a reason the passive voice is used in these cases? Would the example sound better in the active voice?

Find characters

As with active verbs, you can ask students to provide more characters in a draft. They might list all the actors they have identified in a peer's draft, and suggest ways to create more. You can also have students look for the people they see identified in a reading or sample from this book. Are those with more actors easier to follow?

Write concise sentences

Conciseness is a concept, not a method. Students will need continuous work to develop concise writing. Luckily, this is an area where intense work during revision will usually have substantial benefits in terms of improving the quality of the paper overall. If you provide feedback targeting conciseness, and make clear to students how it affects their grade, they will usually be willing to work hard on improving their writing in this way.

Write ethical sentences

You may need to explain to students that avoiding stereotypes isn't just a nicety. From a writer's point of view, it's very poor strategy to risk alienating portions of his or her audience. Then too, in academic, business, and public writing, stereotypes and bias will usually bring swift and often severe repercussions.

Match structure with ideas

Faulty parallelism is a problem that almost all writers end up catching during revision. We tend to use parallelism to order long complex lists, and of course when you compose such lists, you have more time to forget your initial verb or noun form.

Other common problems that can often be identified more readily by reading aloud include misplaced modifiers, subject-verb agreement, and coordination and subordination errors.

Summary for editing sentences

The checklist on page 711 is an excellent reference for you and your students when revising and editing drafts. You can incorporate it into peer review, or refer to it yourself when giving students feedback on their drafts.

Chapter Thirty-one: Avoiding Errors

> Be sure to access the resources available at *MyCompLab* go to (www.mycomplab.com and choose Faigley, *Writing: A Guide to College and Beyond*) to find extensive instruction and practice with grammar and mechanics, as well as ESL instruction and activities.

Chapter goals: This chapter will show students that errors are not insurmountable obstacles. They will learn the appropriate questions to ask about their writing to determine how to avoid errors in final drafts.

Chapter challenges: Error often overwhelms student writers. As an instructor, you have an important role in how students approach error, and the attitude they bring to revision. Prioritizing needed corrections and identifying patterns of error will help your students gain a sense of control over the correctness of their writing.

One good way to make use of this chapter is to have students skim it at the beginning of a project and then, using the checklist on page 719, write a brief list of errors they know they sometimes or often make. After returning their first drafts, have them review their list and this checklist. Do they find there are other areas they need to work on too? Where have they improved? How can they work to improve a certain problem? They can use the chapter's suggestions to plan and execute their revisions.

You and your students can also look for and bring in examples of these errors in books, magazines, and papers. Students take particular pleasure in the "gotcha" mentality of catching pros in errors, and this is a good way for them to sensitize themselves to common writing errors.

Fix fragments

Fixing fragments is often a good way to get students to consider coordination and subordination, since many such errors involve "orphaned" subordinate clauses. Students who have a lot of fragments in their writing may need extra practice constructing sentences with correct subordinate clauses.

Fix run-on sentences

Like fragments, run-ons often occur when a student fails to make clear which parts of a sentence are subordinate to the main clause. One way to help them correct run-ons is to ask them to identify the main idea of the sentence, and then find ways to correctly subordinate, through language and punctuation, the remaining ideas.

Fix comma splices

A comma splice is a common and relatively easy-to-fix form of run-on sentence. Students who have a lot of comma splices in their drafts may benefit from finding and fixing all of them in one sitting. The options available for fixing comma splice are relatively simple and easy to choose from; with some concentrated work, students can usually learn to avoid this error entirely.

Make verbs agree with subjects

Identifying subject-verb agreement problems is usually harder than correcting them. You will likely find yourself marking such errors fairly frequently on drafts, even if students have proofread carefully and reviewed one another's work. Students may need to have these errors pointed out to them several times before they begin to catch them on their own.

Make pronouns agree

The use of "they" as a gender-neutral singular pronoun is now so endemic in spoken English that it sometimes seems pointless to enforce its plural nature in the classroom. Whatever your decision on this issue, your students should understand that singular pronouns must be used for singular subjects, and plural pronouns for plural subjects, to avoid confusing readers.

This is one of those areas of grammar that some students consider "nitpicking." Point out to them that in long sentences or passages with multiple actors, readers can easily lose track of what is happening if pronouns do not agree.

Fix shifts

Shifts in voice, person, and number can seem like small errors, but they often play havoc with readers' comprehension. Explain to your students how easy it is to discourage readers by jarring them with these awkward constructions.

Use modifiers correctly

This is a type of error that often does not interfere excessively with reader comprehension, yet regularly sets instructors' teeth on edge. Point out to your class that, like you, professionals they encounter after college will probably consider these errors much more serious than just the average reader.

Place modifiers carefully

Modifying words and phrases can easily get separated from the words they modify, and lost in the rest of a sentence. This is yet another symptom of a developing writer who has a number of ideas she wants to combine, but lacks the structural tools to combine ideas effectively. Students with lots of modifier problems may benefit from a one-on-one consultation to identify and correct all such errors in a draft in one sitting.

Summary for editing for errors

The checklist on page 719 is an excellent reference for you and your students when revising and editing drafts. You can incorporate it into peer review, or refer to it yourself when giving students feedback on their drafts.

212

Chapter Thirty-two: Understanding Punctuation and Conventions

> Be sure to access the resources available at *MyCompLab* go to
> (www.mycomplab.com and choose Faigley, *Writing: A Guide to College and Beyond*) to find extensive instruction and practice with grammar and mechanics, as well as ESL instruction and activities.

Chapter goals: This chapter will show students that punctuation marks, rather than being a mysterious code devised by English teachers, are really the nuts and bolts they will use to hold their writing together. The instructions given here will help students use punctuation marks correctly, to strengthen their writing.

Chapter challenges: Students can enter college with an astonishing array of "rules" about grammar and punctuation that are counter-intuitive or simply wrong. Often, they have developed overly simplistic writing styles specifically so they don't misuse punctuation. This, of course, inhibits their further development as writers.

Identify where commas are needed

If students are confused about comma placement in a draft, you might ask them to remove all the commas from the troublesome sentence and read it aloud, noting where they naturally pause, and then assessing if commas would be appropriate at those points.

Place commas correctly with modifiers

One common problem with nonrestrictive modifiers is that students will put a comma before them, but not after. Stress to them that interrupting phrases of all kinds require before-*and*-after punctuation, so readers know when they have returned to the main idea of the clause or sentence.

Place commas correctly with clauses and phrases

How long does an introductory phrase need to be before a comma is required? The answer will vary from writer to writer. Give your students some leeway on this issue, as long as the coherence of the writing holds up. More often, students will over-use commas to separate phrases, and your energy will be directed toward reducing unnecessary comma use.

Use semicolons and colons correctly

Student writers can sometimes use semicolons and colons in oddly incongruous ways. Depending on how much reading they have done prior to college, they may not have come across colons, at least not often enough to have a sense of what they are typically used for. They will quickly come to understand the semicolon's value for correcting run-on sentences, but the other uses explained here may seem esoteric to them. But as the complexity of their writing develops, they will come to see how colons and semicolons can help them express complicated thoughts with much-needed structure.

Use hyphens, dashes, and parentheses correctly

Even experienced writers often have to look up correct hyphenation of compound constructions. The rules given here, if memorized, will get the writer out of 90 percent of any hyphenation jams that come up during most projects. If they can't be memorized, however, they can easily be referred to.

The key difference between hyphens and parentheses, structurally, is that hyphens can be used singly or in pairs, while parentheses must open and close. You might have your students consider the difference when a parenthetical phrase is set off with a pair of dashes instead. How does this change the way the phrase fits in with the rest of the sentence?

Use quotation marks correctly

The most common quotation mark error in American college students' writing is the use of single quotation marks where double marks are required. Single quotes, in the United States, are only used within larger quotations. It will probably save you a lot of time if you address this issue with the class as a whole, instead of noting it in one set of rough draft comments after another. This also gives you an opportunity to remind students that (again, in the United States) small punctuation—commas and periods—always goes inside closing quotation marks.

Use other punctuation correctly

Almost any other punctuation error you find in your students' writing is covered in this section of the chapter. You can refer them here when you find specific problems in their drafts involving abbreviations, ellipses, etc.

Understand print conventions

The conventions outlined here are exactly that: conventions. They are not based in any particular logic; there is no specific reason why titles, for example, are italicized rather than placed in bold type. Explain to your students that conventions exist so that every reader, upon seeing a conventional form, automatically perceives the underlying information about the word or phrase (it is a title, it is a foreign word, it is an abbreviation of a longer word). Conventions are very important for guiding writers through writing; memorizing the ones that come up most often will save writers a great deal of time.

Summary for punctuation and conventions

The checklist on page 729 is an excellent reference for you and your students when revising and editing drafts. You can incorporate it into peer review, or refer to it yourself when giving students feedback on their drafts.

Chapter Thirty-three: Writing in a Second Language

> Be sure to access the resources available at *MyCompLab* go to (www.mycomplab.com and choose Faigley, *Writing: A Guide to College and Beyond*) to find extensive instruction and practice with grammar and mechanics, as well as ESL instruction and activities.

Chapter goals: Students writing in a second language should view this chapter as a resource they can refer to throughout the class, for every writing project.

Chapter challenges: Non-native speakers of English face a daunting task when they write in English (a notoriously irregular language). Fortunately, the very act of acquiring a second language gives a writer important skills for effective revision.

Understand how languages differ

As you work with non-native speakers on their writing, plan to spend more time face-to-face discussing their work. They will benefit immensely from time invested this way. It's also a good idea to ask any non-native speakers in your class how much or how little feedback they want on their drafts. They may want you to prioritize the issues they need to work on, and not overwhelm them. Or, they may want you to be very detailed in your comments.

Ask you get to know students, help them devise their own personalized list of reminders based on typical errors in their work. This chapter will help them work through each type of error you are likely to find in their writing.

Understand nouns in English

Article choice for count and non-count nouns is so intuitive to native speakers that most of us cannot even begin to explain how or why we chose a given article. Until non-native speakers gain some fluency and hear or see articles paired with certain words over and over again, they may struggle with article choice. Fortunately, article choice is not an error that interferes grievously with reader comprehension. This is one category of error you may wish to make less of a priority while students focus on other, more critical issues.

Understand articles in English

Compared to count or non-count status, the difference between definite and indefinite is a bit easier to grasp. Still, especially when a student's first language does not use articles, it may take a while for correct article usage to develop as a habit.

Understand verbs and modifiers in English

Tell non-native speakers not to be discouraged by verb and modifier problems. While it would be easy to just write more simply, with fewer modifying phrases, they will advance more quickly as writers in English if they continue to take chances and try to communicate their thoughts completely. Verbs and modifiers in English can be slippery, but with the correct tense, mode, or placement, they allow the writer to express more nuanced ideas.

Understand English sentence structure

You might ask a non-native speaker about conventions in his or her native language—particularly as you look for patterns of error in his or her work. In Japanese, for example, pronoun reference is much looser than what is considered "correct" in English. In other cultures, assertive claims or direct questions may be considered inappropriate in formal writing. Investigating the forms that students have been taught previously can help you see elements of standard written English that native speakers rarely think about.

Summary for second language writers

The checklist on page 739 is an excellent reference for you and your students when revising and editing drafts. You can incorporate it into peer review, or refer to it yourself when giving students feedback on their drafts.

Appendix A: Writing essay exams

In-class essays are a good way to test students' mastery of course content. There is much disagreement in the field of composition, however, as to how well timed essay exams demonstrate students' acquisition of writing skills. For one thing, the kind of writing students do in timed essays is markedly different from the way they are usually asked to write in the classroom—over time, with opportunity for revision. Essay exams also do not mirror especially well the writing process as it usually unfolds in the workplace.

Still, students will take essay exams in other courses, and there are some valuable skills they can learn by preparing for these exams. If essay exams are part of your course, here are some tips for making them useful pedagogically:

- If possible, give students the prompt they will respond to in advance. This makes it easier to write good prompts, since you can bring up topics not every student will automatically have the same level of knowledge about.

- Before the exam, show students some examples of good and poor exam essays, and discuss the qualities of each.

- Consider giving students an opportunity to revise their essay after you have graded it, perhaps for partial credit. This allows them to learn from their mistakes rather than simply regretting them.

- Make your expectations clear in the assignment and provide written criteria you will use to assess the essay. Build these criteria around the reality of the exam. It's never a good idea to count off too heavily for spelling errors on an essay exam.

- Give students a sense of the essay's purpose: Are you assessing their comprehension of course material? Are you testing their ability to argue their point of view persuasively?

Above all, talk to your students about the difference between essay exam writing and writing papers over a two- or three-week period. How are the two activities different? What skills are needed in both situations?

Appendix B: Creating portfolios

If you are using a portfolio system in your writing class, you will ideally already have some sense of its purpose and structure. This appendix of *Writing: A Guide for College and Beyond* gives students information on the basic types of portfolios, and advice on how to fulfill portfolio components. You can refer students to the parts of the appendix that address the type of portfolio you are using.

Whatever kind of portfolio you are using, you must give students all the information they need about it at the very beginning of the semester. Explain how and where drafts will be stored, and when they will be turned in for comments or grades. Note which assignments or assignment types do or do not need to be included in the portfolio. Give them suggestions on how to select pieces for the portfolio.

And most importantly, share with your students the criteria by which portfolios will be judged. These are the goals they will be working toward all semester, so discuss them to make sure they are clear to everyone.